A BARTHOLOMEW MAP & GUIDE

WALK DORSET
& HARDY'S WESSEX

BY DAVID PERROTT AND LAURENCE MAIN

W0009907

JOHN BARTHOLOMEW & SON LTD
EDINBURGH

CONTENTS

We gratefully acknowledge the assistance given by Tom Wightman and The Thomas Hardy Society.

British Library Cataloguing in Publication Data
Perrott, David
  Walk Dorset & Hardy's Wessex
  1. Wessex — Visitors' guides
  I. Title II. Main, Laurence
  914.23
  ISBN 0–7028–0906–3

Published and printed in Scotland by
John Bartholomew & Son Ltd, Duncan Street, Edinburgh EH9 1TA.
First Edition 1989
Copyright © John Bartholomew & Son Ltd, 1989.
ISBN 0 7028 0906 3

Produced for John Bartholomew & Son Ltd by
Perrott Cartographics, Darowen, Machynlleth, Powys SY20 8NS.
Typesetting and litho origination by Litho Link Ltd, Welshpool.

The physical landscape of Britain is changing all the time; eg. as new tracks are made, hedges grubbed up and fields amalgamated. While every care has been taken in the preparation of this guide, neither the authors, Perrott Cartographics nor John Bartholomew & Son Ltd will be responsible for any loss, damage or inconvenience caused by inaccuracies.

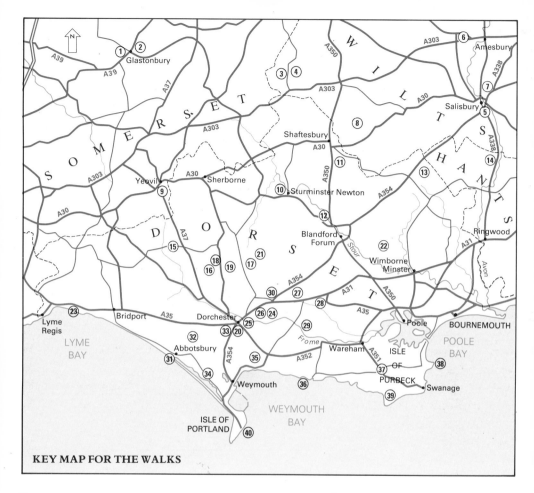

KEY MAP FOR THE WALKS

Key to maps

Scale 1:25000

0   1 mile

0   1 km

All maps are drawn on a north axis, ie. with north at the top

▬▬▬	Major road	+++++	Railway (other)	⣿	Sand
───	Other road	Ⓒ	Description in text	⣿	Woods or forest
– – –	Track or footpath	❋	Viewpoint	554	Spot height in metres
‑ ‑ ‑	Route of walk	▲	Summit	🅿	Parking
+++++	Railway (BR)	⏛⏛	Slope or crags		

WALKING DORSET AND HARDY'S WESSEX

Thomas Hardy was 'convinced that it is better for a writer to know a little bit of the world remarkably well than to know a great part of the world remarkably little'. His little bit of the world, his creation, was Wessex. He first adopted it in *Far from the Madding Crowd*, thus giving a territorial definition, based on the old Saxon kingdom, to unite his series of novels. Hardy's Wessex was always 'partly real, partly dream-country', but it has become a practical definition of a rare thing in England - a province. County boundaries were disregarded, while towns and villages were renamed, often transparently, giving Hardy his *own* stage, upon which his stories were set. He exploited this by demanding of his publishers that the words 'Wessex novels' head the advertising of his booklists. Hardy's Wessex became vividly detailed, making its exploration fascinating.

This book is concerned with the heart of Hardy's Wessex - Dorset and the neighbouring counties of Somerset, Wiltshire and Hampshire. Hardy's map did extend further, from the Scilly Isles to Oxford, but there is enough in this more compact area to be going on with. Lovers of Hardy's novels come here from all over the world on pilgrimages to the shrines of both author and characters. Many more come just to see the beautiful countryside, perhaps ignorant of Hardy and his novels. An awareness of the Wessex novels will add immensely to the appreciation of this area, and allow comparisons to be made between our fairly recent past and the present, whilst enabling the walker, travelling in a way thoroughly recommended by Hardy, to really get to know 'remarkably well' this 'little bit of the world'.

1 EGDON HEATH

The landscape of Hardy's Wessex is far from uniform. Its variety is striking, from the Vale of the Little Dairies to the wilds of Egdon Heath and the inspiring Wessex Heights. Its core is Hardy's native parish of Stinsford (the 'Mellstock' of the novels). Hardy was born here in a cottage at Higher Bockhampton in 1840. This was then a wild, lonely place where 'snakes and efts swarmed in the summer days, and nightly bats would fly about our bedrooms'. The most prominent features of Hardy's boyhood environment were the Heath and the River Frome, which separates Bockhampton from the county town of Dorchester. Hardy gave the individual heaths, which extend to Poole Harbour, the collective name of Egdon Heath, where the outlook was 'lone and bare'. The wild beauty of this excited Hardy's imagination, especially in *The Return of the Native*, where Clym Yeobright 'was permeated with its scenes, with its substance, and with its odours'. In *The Mayor of Casterbridge*, Hardy described the heath as 'that ancient country whose surface never had been stirred to a finger's depth, save by the scratching of rabbits, since brushed by the feet of the earliest tribes'.

Only small pockets of this wasteland have survived the agricultural improvements and the dense conifer afforestation of the 20th century, when few seem capable of appreciating the value of such wilderness. One of the few, Christopher Booker, in a letter to *The Times* (20th February, 1982) pointed out that 'this strange and unique fragment of Britain's landscape is as irreplaceable as a Gothic cathedral'. Wildlife that survives in the remaining habitats includes the lovely marsh gentian, the smooth snake and the sand lizard. The heath is a valuable habitat, with geology, climate, soil-structure and vegetation combining to form a rare character.

2 THE VALLEY OF THE GREAT DAIRIES

The River Frome flows eastwards to Poole Harbour. Its green, fertile valley was where the waters 'were as clear as the pure River of Life shown to the Evangelist, rapid as the shadow of a cloud, with pebbly shallows that prattled to the sky all day long'. Angel Clare courted Tess here, in the valley her spirits up wonderfully' upon first sight. This is still lush, dairy-farming landscape, although the milkmaids have been replaced by machines. Summer brings a leafy arborescence, but in the early morning, Hardy noted 'perhaps the summer fog was more general, and the meadows lay like a white sea, out of which the scattered trees rose like dangerous rocks'. Here was a rich seam from which Hardy could link the environment with human emotions, as in 'Tess of the d'Urbervilles': 'Amid the oozing fatness and warm ferments of the Froom Vale, at a season when the rush of juices could almost be heard below the hiss of fertilization, it was impossible that the most fanciful love should not grow passionate. The ready bosoms existing there were impregnated by their surroundings'. In autumn the river filled up and 'the smallest gullies were all full; there was no taking short cuts anywhere, and foot passengers were compelled to follow the permanent ways'.

3 THE VALE OF THE LITTLE DAIRIES

The Vale of Blackmore, or Blackmoor, was the home of Tess. It is best seen from the surrounding heights, as from Dogbury Hill. Its gateway is Sturminster Newton, past which flows the River Stour. This river and its tributaries give the vale its character, enhanced by the villages which cluster on islands of higher ground above land liable to flooding. Hardy wrote in *The Woodlanders* that the Vale 'cannot be regarded as inferior to any inland scenery of the sort in the west of England, or perhaps anywhere in the Kingdom'. The heavy clay soil is the kind where Hardy felt 'superstitions linger longest'. The trees relate to humans, as in *The Woodlanders*, when Marty South remarked that the young pines she was planting seemed to 'sigh because they are very sorry to begin life in earnest - just as we be.'

4 SOMERSET

Hardy knew south Somerset well. He lived at Yeovil for a few months in 1876 and explored the surrounding countryside. The contrast between Somerset and Dorset is great, with the clay of the Somerset Levels replacing the chalk and limestone of Dorset. Here is the Vale of Avalon and Glastonbury

Tor, a place of the highest significance in its own right. Perhaps this intimidated Hardy as he confined himself to poetry in this county, finding inspiration for what is said to be his most successful poem, *The Trampwoman's Tragedy*:

'Beneath us figured tor and lea,
From mendip to the western sea -
I doubt if finer sight there be
Within this royal realm.'

5 THE CHANNEL COAST

Hardy's Wessex is not just magnificent countryside, it also has fine coastal scenery. Weymouth was only 10 miles (16 km) from Hardy's home and the novelist was fond of 'the boats, the sands, the esplanade'. Hardy wrote *Desperate Remedies*, his first published novel, in Weymouth, but *The Trumpet Major* and *The Dynasts* are the fruits of a longer association with the coast. Hardy's grandparents remembered when this coastline was under threat of invasion by Napoleon and folk-memories and legends from that time enliven Hardy's works. *The Hand of Ethelberta* is the novel of Purbeck. This 'isle' is a microcosm of the Dorset landscape, with chalk, clay, limestone, sand and shale, rugged and gentle scenery. It is reached through the gap guarded by Corfe Castle which, like the cliffs and headlands of Purbeck, was visited frequently by Hardy. The newly-married Thomas and Emma Hardy walked the cliffs east of Swanage, where the detached stumps of chalk stand witness to the power of the waves. Further west, towards Weymouth, the spectacular cove at Lulworth is where Sergeant Troy was thought to have drowned in *Far from the Madding Crowd*. This military connection is reinforced by the figure of George III on horseback carved in the chalk above Osmington, as if the king were reviewing his troops (the downs were the venue of grand military reviews in Napoleonic times). Across the bay is Portland, the peninsula 'carved by Time out of a single stone'. This is a place of prison-warders, quarrymen and the Services, crowded together as described in *The Well-Beloved*. The cliffs of Portland offer a splendid view of Chesil Bank, stretching west towards Abbotsbury Swannery. Inland is the Hardy monument - to Nelson's Hardy (Sir Thomas Masterman Hardy), not the novelist. The cliffs reach their climax near the Devon border with Golden Cap the highest cliff on the Channel coast.

6 WILTSHIRE AND HAMPSHIRE

Salisbury, the 'Melchester' of Hardy's novels, was his favourite city. It is divided from Dorset by Cranborne Chase, 'a country of ragged woodland, which, though intruded on by the plough at places, remained largely intact from prehistoric times, and still abounded with yews of gigantic growth and oaks tufted with mistletoe'. This was the symbolic background for the violent episodes in Tess's life, its 'Druidical mistletoe' heralding the concluding scene at Stonehenge. The Chase itself made Tess 'restless and uneasy' where 'she feared the unknown'. Wardour Castle, on the northern edge of the Chase, is the destination of an outing by Jude and Sue in *Jude the Obscure*. The couple were taking a trip from Salisbury, where the Training College had been attended in real life by Hardy's sister Mary and in *Jude the Obscure* by Sue Bridehead. Hardy, the trained architect, found Salisbury's cathedral close 'as beautiful a scene as any I know in England - or for the matter of that elsewhere'.

7 WESSEX HEIGHTS

There are no mountains in Wessex, but there are high places with magnificent views. These were Hardy's Wessex Heights, 'where men have never cared to haunt nor women have walked with me, and ghosts then keep their distance; and I know some liberty'. The north Dorset escarpment overlooking the Vale of Blackmore constantly recurs in the novels. Here is the scene of Tess's poverty stricken winter at Flintcombe-Ash, 'a starve-acre place' where 'Tess slaved in the morning frosts and in the afternoon rains'. Not far from here is the giant of Cerne Abbas, the 'Cernel Giant' who ate babies in ancient times according to Mrs Cantle in *The Dynasts*. This is also sheep country and Hardy wrote of the sheep-fair at 'Greenhill' (Woodbury Hill) outside 'Kingsbere' (Bere Regis), the annual gathering on the top of a hill attended by 'multitude after multitude' of 'horned and hornless' sheep. Nearby is Tolpuddle, the home of the trade union

Martyrs. Their trial was held in Dorchester, Hardy's 'Casterbridge' and the town most closely associated with the novelist. The Dorset County Museum provides a fine introduction to the area.

8 WESSEX IN HISTORY AND LEGEND

There was another Wessex which existed long before that of Thomas Hardy. It is conventionally ascribed to the West Saxons, who established themselves in the 6th century in the area south of the River Thames, including much of the modern counties of Avon, Somerset, Dorset, Wiltshire, Hampshire and Berkshire. Their leader was Cerdic of the Gewissae, however, a British king regaining his patrimony.

The most famous son of the house of Wessex was Alfred the Great, who was markedly Celtic in outlook. His chosen adviser was Asser, a Welsh monk whose brother, Morgan Hen, was king of south Wales. Alfred's mentor in his youth was St Swithin, derived from Sywedydd, meaning magician, or druid.

The landscape of Wessex is littered with ancient monuments, with Stonehenge arguably the most famous in the world. Agriculture in Wessex has been dated back to 4000 BC, although there were cave dwellers here in the middle of the Ice Age, about half a million years ago. By about 500 BC, much of what was to become Wessex was the tribal territory of the Durotriges, who built impressive hillforts, such as that at Maiden Castle, just outside Dorchester. They could not stop the Romans however, who established their culture here for 400 years. The British Hillfort of Old Sarum, near Salisbury, was converted into a Roman town, but Maiden Castle was abandoned in favour of a new town called Durnovaria, which became Dorchester, Hardy's 'Casterbridge'.

9 WILDLIFE

The variety in the Wessex landscape is reflected in its wildlife. The fragments of heathland left in Dorset are home to many rare plants and animals. In summer you may see an emperor dragonfly, or a silver studded blue butterfly. The smooth snake, one of Britain's rarest reptiles, has its home on the open heathland, while a marsh gentian may be seen amidst thicker vegetation. On the limestone cliffs, in summer, look out for the adonis blue butterfly. Gulls, including kittiwakes, abound along the coast, with Portland Bill being a major bird migration point. The spring or autumn would be the best time to witness this spectacle. In summer, the swans can be seen at Abbotsbury. Poole Harbour is a feeding ground for many birds, including a large colony of black-headed gulls.

10 RIGHTS OF WAY

These walks are along rights of way. Please remember to keep to the path and always regard it as a privilege to follow it across someone else's land; in that way we can build an atmosphere of co-operation, rather than confrontation, in the countryside. Many of these walks cross land grazed by sheep, where dogs are not welcome. The Animals Act (1971) states that dogs endangering livestock may be shot. The Protection of Livestock Act (1953) makes it an offence to permit a dog to worry livestock, with a maximum penalty of £200. Worrying includes being at large in a field in which there are sheep. Wessex provides relatively easy walking country, but walking boots or stout walking shoes are still recommended, as is a good anorak with a hood. If your path is obstructed (although these routes were chosen for their lack of obstructions), contact the county council, which is the highway authority. In Dorset, you are also advised to contact the lively local Ramblers' Association, whose Hon. Secretary is Miss P.N. Houston, MBE, Old Post Cottage, Ibberton, Blandford, Dorset, DT11 OEN (Tel 02586 444). Further information on rights of way is available from the Ramblers' Association, 1-5 Wandsworth Road, London, SW8 2LJ (Tel 01-582 6878).

11 THE COUNTRY CODE

Enjoy the countryside and respect its life and work.
Guard against all risk of fire.
Leave gates as you find them.
Keep your dogs under close control.
Keep to public paths across farmland.
Use gates and stiles to cross fences, hedges and walls.
Leave livestock, crops and machinery alone.
Take your litter home.
Help to keep all water clean. Protect wildlife, plants and trees.
Take special care on country roads.
Make no unnecessary noise.

12 USEFUL ADDRESSES

Telephone 0898 141207 for a local weather forecast. Car parking information is given at the start of each walk, and it is also possible to reach the start of many by public transport. British Rail's scenic line between Salisbury and Yeovil Junction is useful, while rural buses (some of the vintage variety) run everywhere. Services are infrequent to many places, however, so it is advisable to obtain the annual booklet 'Public Transport in Rural Dorset' (published in April) from the Transportation and Engineering Dept, Dorset County Council, County Hall, Dorchester, Dorset, DT1 1XJ (Tel 0305 25100). You may need to re-check these timetables locally in the summer. Frequent services on the urban fringe (particularly near Weymouth) are not included. Details of these and of bus services outside Dorset should be obtained from local Tourist Information Centres and the bus companies:
Southern National, 80 Esplanade, Weymouth, Dorset, DT4 7AA. Tel. (0305) 783645.
Wilts & Dorset, Bus Station, Endless Street, Salisbury, SP1 1DW, Wiltshire. Tel (0722) 336855.
Wilts & Dorset, Bus Station, Arndale Centre, Poole, Dorset, BH15 1SN. Tel (0202) 673555.
Badgerline Ltd, Badger House, Oldmixon Crescent, Weston-super-Mare, Avon, BS24 9AX. Tel (0934) 416171.
Wessex is divided between two tourist boards:
Southern Tourist Board
The Old Town Hall, Leigh Road, Eastleigh, Hampshire, SO5 4DE. Tel (0703) 616027.
West Country Tourist Board
37 Southernhay East, Exeter, Devon, EX1 1QS. Tel (0392) 76351.

The Thomas Hardy Society
c/o Mr J. Maybery, 'Copper Trees', Salston Ride, Ottery St Mary, Devon, EX11 1RH. Tel (040481) 3032.

Walk 1
WEARYALL HILL
4 miles (6.4 km) Moderate

Wearyall Hill is thought by many to be the home of the Holy Thorn, the sanctity of which was said to be recognised even by the animal kingdom. One old Somerset legend tells of a man making a pilgrimage to it and returning with a single thorn which he planted near his home. It soon grew and the villagers were amazed to witness all the farm animals gathering around it just before midnight on Christmas Eve, accompanied by the pilgrim. At the stroke of midnight, under the light of a full moon, the beasts knelt to the Holy Thorn, now in blossom. Hardy based a poem on this tale.

"If someone said on Christmas Eve
'Come; see the oxen kneel
In the lonely barton by yonder combe
Our childhood used to know,'
I should go with him in the gloom,
Hoping it might be so."
This, then, is a walk across holy ground.

A History, myth and legend are entwined on Wearyall Hill. The thorn tree here is believed to be one of several descendants of the original Holy Thorn which survive in Glastonbury, said to mark the spot where Joseph of Arimathea planted his staff. It took root and burst into flower, thus signalling the end of the saint's long journey. A puritan fanatic cut the original tree down, but not before it had provided cuttings. It is considered significant that Joseph's weary band halted on Wearyall Hill, which represents a 'fish', the symbol for Pisces, in the Glastonbury Zodiac (field patterns which outline the signs of the Zodiac, when seen from high above).

Wearyall Hill also symbolises the Celtic Salmon of Wisdom and is the King Fisherman's Castle of Arthurian legend. Joseph was the old Fisher-King, arriving as a key-witness to the Resurrection at a time when the local Silures king, Arviragus, was under pressure from the Romans, who had just massacred the druids in Anglesey. Arviragus recognised the title of the resurrected 'Salmon of Knowledge' by granting Joseph the 12 Hides (or 12 Hidden Figures) of the Zodiac) at Glastonbury.

Joseph was also a tin-trader. Tin is the metal of Jupiter, which is the ruling planet of Pisces. Joseph's association with this area was a long one. Many believe he sailed with Anne, the British princess, to Palestine, where she gave birth to the Virgin Mary. Jesus is thought by many to have come here with his uncle to visit his relations. He was also recognised by the druids as the promised and expected god Esse.

B Pons Perilis, or Pomparles Bridge, is the Perilous Bridge of Arthurian legend. Here the initiate passed from life to death to rebirth, in a supreme test of courage.

C Notice the stone marking the site of St Bride's well. This Celtic saint lived nearby at Old Beckery.

D In one old Somerset legend, King Arthur was commanded by an angel to go to the hermitage on Beckery Knoll. This was a place of pilgrimage because St Bride had lived there. He was offered the body of the Christ-child by Mary herself. He consumed the Holy Child, who reappeared whole on the altar.

E The canal that crossed the river here was opened in 1833, but closed in 1854.

F Paradise allotments should be fertile. This was the town's septic pond in the Middle Ages.

G Glastonbury Abbey lies between the Zodiac signs for Pisces and Aquarius. The abbey was built over the original wattle church, said to have been built by Jesus and restored by Joseph of Arimathea. Encased in lead, for protection, by St David in 546, it was destroyed by a fire in 1184. The tomb of 'Arthur', dug up by the monks in 1191 (at Henry II's behest) was actually that of Prince Iestyn, the 11th-century traitor prince of South Wales.

Walk 1
WEARYALL HILL
Continued

0   1 mile

0   1 km

6 *When you reach an old bridge that used to carry the now dismantled Somerset and Dorset Railway ('the dear old S & D - Slow & Dirty') across the River Brue, look first for stone walls in the bank downstream. These show where an aqueduct used to take canal barges over the river by means of locks. Cross over the old railway bridge. Turn left immediately to a gate, then right to follow the course of the old canal.*

7 *Go ahead through a gate to a lane and continue through the gate opposite. Walk with the course of the old canal still on your right. Cross a footbridge ahead and continue to cross a stile beside a gate. Turn right along a lane, bear left over a bridge and turn left up a waymarked path.*

8 *Go ahead over the line of the dismantled railway through a gate. Keep to the right-hand edge of the field to reach a footbridge over a stream ahead. Continue past allotment gardens and turn right along a path to Benedict Street. Turn left to reach the Market Cross and turn right up Magdalene Street back to the car park on your left.*

1 *Start from the car park at the entrance to Glastonbury Abbey, which is next to the Town Hall in Magdalene Street. Buses (376 from Yeovil and Bristol) also stop here.*
Turn left, then right at the A39 to Street.

2 *Turn left through the swing gate waymarked 'Wearyall Hill'. Veer right uphill to a stile in the hedge at the top.* **Don't cross it!** *Turn right along the ridge path, passing the Holy Thorn. Admire the views, which include Exmoor, the Quantocks and the Mendips. Go ahead to a stile and continue past houses on your left. Look for a stile on your left.*

3 *Cross onto the road and turn right. Bear left along Roman Way and cross the A39, just before Pons Perilis. (Pomparles Bridge).*

4 *Go over a waymarked stile to walk with the River Brue on your left. Look for the stone marking the site of St Bride's Well.*

5 *Turn left over a bridge and walk with the river now on your right.*

Glastonbury

New Close Farm

A39

Wearyall Hill

Northover

River Brue

A39

(E) (F) (P)(G) (D) (C) (A) (B)

Walk 2
GLASTONBURY TOR
2.5 miles (4 km) Moderate

Hardy visited Glastonbury on at least three occasions. In 1902 it was the destination of the cycle ride during which he composed the *Trampwoman* poem. The trampwoman's friend, Mother Lee, died here. In 1904 he cycled to Glastonbury again to spend 'a romantic day or two among the ruins'. In 1924 he witnessed the musical version of his verse-play *The Queen of Cornwall* at the Glastonbury Festival. 'Glaston' may have been in Hardy's Outer Wessex, but it is a central point for seekers of the mystical new age of Aquarius. The Glastonbury Zodiac symbolises Aquarius as a phoenix, taking wing from Glastonbury.

2 *Opposite St John the Baptist Church, turn right down a lane to Silver Street. Continue to Lambrook Street and turn right as it becomes Chilkwell Street. Turn left up Dod Lane and go straight on when the road bends left.*

3 *Cross a waymarked stile and walk uphill. Glastonbury Tor soon comes into view ahead above the hedge on your right. Continue through a waymarked kissing-gate and along a lane to a waymarked stile in the corner ahead.*

4 *Cross the stile to walk with the hedge on your left to a stile ahead. Turn half-right to reach a stile giving access to a lane below the Tor. Turn left along the lane, ignoring a lane on your left, to a waymarked stile beside a gate on your right.*

1 *Start from the car park at the entrance to Glastonbury Abbey, which is next to the Town Hall in Magdalene Street. Buses (376 from Yeovil and Bristol) also stop here.*
Turn right past the Town Hall to Market Place, with its Cross. Turn right up High Street to the Parish Church of St John the Baptist.

6 *Turn left to Chilkwell Street, where you turn right. After 30 yards (27 m), you will see the Chalice Well on your right. Continue along Chilkwell Street to a fork, where you can visit the Somerset Rural Life Museum on your left before continuing up Bere Lane and turning right along Fisher's Hill back to the start.*

5 *Cross the stile and follow the clear path to the summit of the Tor. Walk beside a hedge on your right to a stile, then bear right up steps. Continue along the path on the other side of the summit, down towards Glastonbury. Cross a stile in a hedge near the bottom and go ahead to a stile leading to Wellhouse Lane.*

A Visit the Glastonbury Tribunal to see the find from the prehistoric Glastonbury Lake Village.

B St John's Church has the Holy Thorn tree in its churchyard from which sprigs are sent each Christmas to the Queen and Queen Mother.

C Glastonbury Tor was thought to be in William Blake's mind when he wrote
'And did those feet in ancient time
Walk upon England's mountains green?'

D The Chalice Well is held in the beak of the phoenix - the Aquarian Water-Carrier. Joseph of Arimathea is said to have hidden the chalice containing Christ's blood here. The water is stained crimson by algae floating in it.

E The Somerset Rural Life Museum is housed in the old abbey barn.

F Glastonbury Abbey is believed to have been built on the site of the wattle church built by Jesus Himself.

Walk 3
ALFRED'S TOWER
5 miles (8 km) Easy

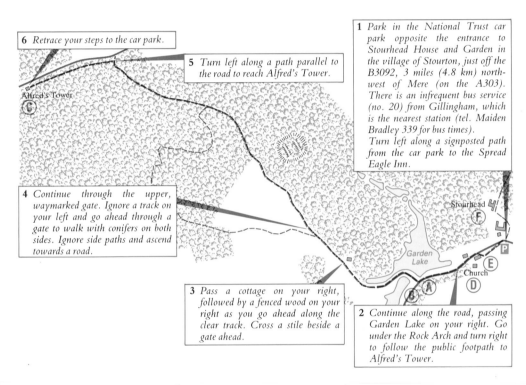

6 Retrace your steps to the car park.

5 Turn left along a path parallel to the road to reach Alfred's Tower.

Alfred's Tower

C

4 Continue through the upper, waymarked gate. Ignore a track on your left and go ahead through a gate to walk with conifers on both sides. Ignore side paths and ascend towards a road.

3 Pass a cottage on your right, followed by a fenced wood on your right as you go ahead along the clear track. Cross a stile beside a gate ahead.

1 Park in the National Trust car park opposite the entrance to Stourhead House and Garden in the village of Stourton, just off the B3092, 3 miles (4.8 km) north-west of Mere (on the A303). There is an infrequent bus service (no. 20) from Gillingham, which is the nearest station (tel. Maiden Bradley 339 for bus times).
Turn left along a signposted path from the car park to the Spread Eagle Inn.

Stourhead **F**

Garden Lake

Church

E

D

A

B

2 Continue along the road, passing Garden Lake on your right. Go under the Rock Arch and turn right to follow the public footpath to Alfred's Tower.

A This rock arch carries visitors to Stourhead Gardens over the public road.

B Notice the Cascade, which was engineered in 1766.

C Alfred's Tower gives fine views over Somerset, Dorset and Wiltshire. Hardy named it 'Stourton Tower' and alluded to it in his poem *Molly Gone*. Henry Hoare, the enthusiast antiquarian respon-sible for what we now see at Stourhead, was reading about Alfred the Great in Voltaire's *L'Histoire Générale* when he decided to crown his scheme with a tower on Kingsettle Hill. It is 160 feet (48 m) high and was designed by Henry Flitcroft. It is open from 2 to 5 on Wednesdays, Thursdays, Saturdays and Sundays from April to October.

D St Peter's Church, Stourton, dates from at least the 13th century.

E The Spread Eagle Inn.

F Stourhead House is open to the public from 2 to 6 daily (except Friday) from May to September, and from Saturday to Wednesday in April and October.

11

Walk 4
WHITE SHEET HILL
4.5 miles (7.2 km) Easy

This is a straightforward route to a fine viewpoint overlooking Wiltshire, Dorset and Somerset. It links with Walk 3 (Alfred's Tower) and with a visit to Stourhead. A wide, clear track leads over the chalk downland to an ancient hill fort which is now in a nature reserve. Here, at a height of 810 feet (246 m), our ancestors established themselves above the thickly forested lowlands.

1 Park in the National Trust car park opposite the entrance to Stourhead House and Garden in the village of Stourton, just off the B3092, 3 miles (4.8 km) northwest of Mere (on the A303). There is an infrequent bus service (no. 20) from Gillingham, which is the nearest station (tel. Maiden Bradley 339 for bus times).
Turn right when facing the entrance to Stourhead House and walk back towards the B3092 road.

3 When you reach a house on your left, turn right through a gate up a hedged track. Ignore side tracks and walk uphill towards trees. Go ahead through a gate to walk with the hedge on your left to another gate. Continue uphill with a fence on your right. Ignore a stile on your right and a lane on your left, but cross a stile ahead into the nature reserve.

4 Follow a fence on your right uphill to a stile ahead. Cross this and bear right, passing two disc barrows on your right. Go ahead to the triangulation point (O.S. pillar) opposite the T.V. mast on the Iron Age earthwork of White Sheet Castle.

2 At the crossroads just before the B3092, turn left up an old road. Continue along the B3092.

5 Retrace your steps to the start.

A Stourhead House is in the care of the National Trust and deserves a visit. It was built in the 1720's by Henry Hoare I, the banker son of a Lord Mayor of London, and contains some fine Chippendale furniture. The glorious gardens were created by Henry Hoare II, who returned from his Grand Tour in 1741 determined to change his corner of Wiltshire into a Classical landscape, as found in Italy. The River Stour was dammed, while a large lake was made out of medieval fish-ponds. Deciduous and coniferous trees were planted to provide a variety of shades, which contrasted with the brilliant colours of daffodils, bluebells, rhododendrons and azaleas.

B The small, oval, earthwork on your left as you cross the final stile is of Neolithic (New Stone Age) date, being constructed in about 2500 BC. It may have been a gathering place and a religious site rather than a fortified settlement.

C White Sheet Castle is an Iron Age hill-fort. A single rampart and ditch sufficed on its south and west sides, where there are steep slopes giving natural protection, but three banks and ditches are present on the north and east sides, facing the level plateau. There is also a cross-dyke 440 yards (400 m) to the north. White Sheet refers to the steep, chalky slope of this hillside.

Walk 5
SALISBURY (MELCHESTER)
3 miles (4.8 km) Easy

```
0                                                    1 mile
|----|----|----|----|----|----|----|----|----|----|
0                              1 km
```

Salisbury is Hardy's 'Melchester'. It was 'a quiet and soothing place, almost wholly ecclesiastical in its tone; a spot where worldly learn- ing and intellectual smartness had no establishment'.

1 Start from Salisbury's main car park, which is signposted off Castle Street.
Walk back to the river and walk towards the city centre with the river on your left, and the cathedral spire ahead.

2 Turn left to the church of St Thomas Becket. Follow the lane on the left of the church to Blue Boar Row. Notice the execution plaque by Debenham's and the second Georgian house from the Endless Street end.

3 Turn right across the Market Square. Turn right past the Guildhall and walk along Ox Row. Turn left in the corner to the Poultry Cross. Turn right, then left down High Street. Pass under an arch towards the cathedral.

4 Turn right to Mompesson House, then left down West Walk past the Regimental Museum and the Salisbury and South Wiltshire Museum.

5 Turn left towards the west door of the cathedral, then bear right along Broad Walk to go through an arched gateway (shut from 10 pm. to 7.30 am.) on your left to De Vaux Place.

6 Turn right along Nicholas Road to cross the Avon and bear right up Harnham Road, passing the Rose and Crown pub on your right. Continue past All Saints church on your right.

7 Fork right down Lower Street. Turn right at the signpost to the 'city centre' along the Town Path. Pass the Old Mill Hotel on your left as you cross the Nadder. Constable painted his famous picture of the cathedral from the Town Path.

8 Cross a footbridge to Queen Elizabeth Gardens. Bear right across a second footbridge and turn left to Crane Bridge Road. Turn left after the bridge to walk with the Avon on your left.

9 Cross the road to enter the Maltings and walk with the river now on your right back to the car park.

A St Thomas Becket's church was the scene of Sue's wedding to Phillotson in *Jude the Obscure*.

B This plaque commemorates the execution of Henry, Duke of Buckingham, in 1483, for rebelling against King Richard III.

C The second Georgian house along Blue Boar Row from Endless Street is probably the original of the Harnham's house in *On the Western Circuit*.

D The Guildhall is Hardy's 'Town Hall' where Ethelberta attended Christopher's concert in 'a large upstair assembly room' (the Banqueting Room).

E The Poultry Cross dates from the 15th century.

F Mompesson House is a Queen Anne town house of 1701, in the care of the National Trust. It is renowned for its elegant plaster-work ceilings.

G The Duke of Edinburgh's Royal Regiment Museum.

H The excellent Salisbury and South Wiltshire Museum is housed in the King's House (where Richard III slept). This used to form part of the college where Sue (in *Jude the Obscure*) and Hardy's sisters trained to be teachers.

I The cathedral – Hardy called it 'the most graceful architectural pile in England'.

Walk 6
STONEHENGE
7 miles (11.2 km) Easy

This is a walk along a ley line past one of the most famous of Bronze Age cemeteries, and the climax of a visit to Stonehenge makes this a special walk for anyone interested in our distant past. Hardy realised the drama of the scenery and made Stonehenge the conclusion of Tess's flight with Angel after the killing of Alec d'Urberville. Here, Tess appeared as the ritual sacrifice, fulfilling her own prophecy: 'Once victim, always victim - that's the law!' As Tess slept, Angel watched the black cloud of night lift 'like the lid of a pot, letting in at the earth's edge the coming day....The band of silver paleness along the east horizon made even the distant parts of the Great Plain appear dark and near; and the whole enormous landscape bore that impress of reserve, taciturnity, and hesitation which is usual just before day.'

If you rely on public transport, you may prefer to take a bus to Amesbury and start on Stonehenge Road (see direction 6) as there is only an infrequent bus service to Stonehenge (no. 3 from Salisbury). The path through the wood near direction 4 may be muddy in wet weather, but the wood itself is a haven for wildlife.

A This old straight track is one of the leys or earth-energy lines that converge at Stonehenge. It continues straight ahead from Stonehenge when our path bends left after 1 mile (1.6 km).

B The round barrows on both sides of the track are the Bronze Age burial mounds of Normanton Down. One barrow (at the western end of the line) was excavated in 1808 and found to contain a skeleton of a 'tall and stout man', a bronze axe, a spearhead, a dagger (the wooden dagger handle was decorated with tiny gold pins), a gold breastplate, a belt hook and a polished stone macehead with an elaborately decorated handle.

C Three ley lines cross at this disc barrow.

D Stonehenge is the most famous prehistoric monument in Britain, if not in the world. It was started 5000 years ago and the reason for its construction has been lost in the mists of time. There have been countless explanations proffered, however, while the site has been the object of all kinds of research. The major axis of Stonehenge was definitely aligned with the sun at the summer and winter solstices. The erection of the stones was also a major operation. Most of the larger stones were brought 20 miles (32 km) from Fyfield Down, near Marlborough. The smaller Bluestones were brought from the Preseli Mountains of Dyfed. If the mind boggles at the thought of such prehistoric organisation, consider the task of erecting them once on site - the larger stones weigh over 50 tons each. Massive stone lintels were mortice-and-tenoned to these uprights and are curved to follow the circumference of a circle.

The name is of Saxon origin, meaning 'hanging stones', referring to its stone lintels, which make this unique among the stone circles of Albion. About half of its original stones are missing but the plan is clear. An outer circle of 30 sarsens (supporting lintels) encloses a circle of Bluestones (about 60 originally). Inside this are five sarsen 'trilithons' (two uprights supporting a horizontal lintel) arranged in a horseshoe shape, with its open end towards the north-east, where the midsummer sun rises. Then there is an inner horseshoe of Bluestones (19 originally). The 'Altar Stone' lies at the apex of the horseshoe. The 'Slaughter Stone' lies on the midsummer sun axis on the causeway which breaks the bank and ditch encircling the monument at this crucial point. Also near this axis but further out, almost on the modern perimeter fence and the A344, stands the 'Heel Stone'. Stonehenge is open daily (admission charge).

0   1 mile
0   1 km

1 Start from the car park at Stonehenge, on the A344, 2 miles (3.2 km) west of Amesbury. Turn right along the A344, then turn left up a fenced track to the A303. Turn left to reach a waymarked gate on your right. Walk away from Stonehenge down a fenced track.

5 Turn right to walk with the fence on your left. Pass a chalk pit crowned by a disc barrow on your right. Turn left at the end of this field and go through a kissing-gate beside a gate to walk along a fenced track which bends left as it climbs. Cross a track to go through a gate ahead signposted 'Amesbury 1'. Walk down to a signposted gate and a footbridge over the Avon.

6 Cross a second footbridge to go ahead past houses on your left and a cemetery on your right, to emerge at Stonehenge Road. Turn left to reach the A303. Fork right along the A344 back to Stonehenge and the car park.

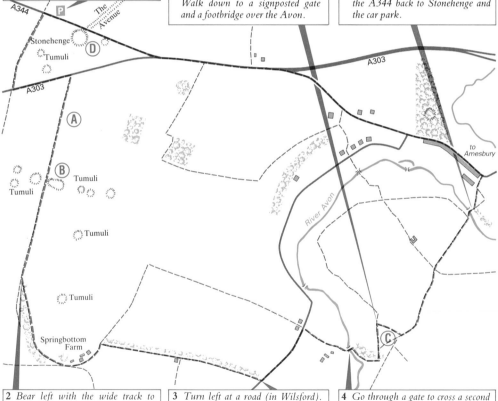

2 Bear left with the wide track to walk with trees across the field on your right. Ignore a track from the right, but keep left to a farm. Bear left along the farm track before bending right with it.

3 Turn left at a road (in Wilsford). Walk to Normenton and turn right at the post-box to walk down a gated and fenced lane. Just before the end of this lane, turn left over a stile beside a gate and bear right, ignoring stiles on your right, to reach a footbridge over the Avon.

4 Go through a gate to cross a second footbridge and bear right into a wood. The path goes beside a stream on your left to a footbridge. Cross this and turn left. Follow a track to a gate ahead, but **don't go through it!**

Walk 7
OLD SARUM
4.5 miles (7.2 km) Easy

Old Sarum was Hardy's 'Old Melchester'. In his day it was heavily overgrown and swarmed with rabbits. Its deep ditch was filled with trees, which provided cover for Anna's seduction in *On the Western Circuit*. There are still trees on the slopes of Old Sarum, but English Heritage keep the grass mown around its fascinating ruins, notably the outline of the old cathedral. Its bishop was responsible for moving the cathedral and town to a new site 2 miles (3.2 km) to the south. The route between Old and New Sarum now provides a delightful riverside walk and a chance to follow the footsteps of the Roman legions along Ackling Dyke. This walk can be combined with Walk 5.

A Old Sarum was originally an Iron Age hill fort. It remained in continuous habitation, however, with Romans, Saxons, Danes and Normans living behind its ramparts and earthworks. William the Conqueror inspected his victorious army here in 1070. His nephew, Bishop Osmund (later St Osmund), built a castle and a cathedral, but just five days after the cathedral's consecration in 1078 it was struck by lightning and largely destroyed. The nave survived to be incorporated into Bishop Roger's restored cathedral. It remained an unhappy site for such an ecclesiastical building, however. Roger had also built a castle which was to serve as the bishop's palace, but the proximity of the civil and religious authorities led to antagonism. A lack of water was a problem, and gave the clergy an excuse to move to a home of their own. The wind was bitterly criticised, while it was claimed that 'the whiteness of the chalk causes blindness'. No one disputed Bishop Poore when he said that a vision of the Blessed Virgin told him to build at a certain place which local people would direct him to. This proved to be the site of the present Salisbury cathedral, 2 miles (3.2 km) to the south in the unpromising wetland near the river. Work on building the new cathedral started in 1220 and the bishop moved to New Sarum in 1226. The body of St Osmund was removed to a shrine within the new building. To King Alfred the Great is attributed the saying 'there is nothing in that which men say, to wit, that a thing happens by chance'. Considering the history of the removal of Old Sarum's cathedral to modern Salisbury, how strange it is to discover that both sites are on one of the classic examples of a ley line. An alignment was first noticed by Sir Norman Lockyer and Alfred Watkins quoted it in *The Old Straight Track* (published 1925). Later researchers, notably Paul Devereux, have marginally changed the ley's angle and confirmed an 18 mile (29 km) alignment which starts at a tumulus north of Stonehenge, strikes the edge of the earthwork of Stonehenge just where it meets the Avenue (leys often strike the edges of earthworks rather than going through their centres) and continues to Old Sarum. There is a fine view of it running south from the ruins of the Norman castle towards Salisbury Cathedral, where the ley passes just to the east of the spire and on to the north-west corner of the earthworks of Clearbury Ring. It continues south of this wooded Iron Age camp to Frankenbury Camp, east of Fordingbridge.

B Old Sarum was the Sorviodunum of the Romans. This path is on the line of Ackling Dyke, the Roman road from Exeter via Dorchester and Badbury Rings. It met other Roman roads from Winchester, Silchester and the Mendips at Old Sarum.

C Near this spot beneath the spreading branches of an elm tree the Members of Parliament for the Borough of Old Sarum were in former times elected, most notable of whom was William Pitt, afterwards Earl of Chatham. This borough was abolished in 1832.

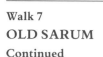
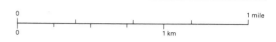

0   1 mile
0   1 km

5 *Turn right along the fenced track. Go through a gate and bear right to visit Old Sarum. Continue along the path down towards the main road.*

4 *Turn right up a farm track. Maintain your direction when you reach a road at its bend.*

6 *Just before the road, turn right along the signposted footpath, with the hedge on your right. Fork left along the hedged track at the end of the first field. Ignore a stile on your right before the Parliament Tree stone.*

Old Sarum

Castle

Castle Hill

A345

Parsonage Farm

(A)

(B)

(C)

7 *Go straight on at the corner of a road to a signposted footpath on your left as the road bends right. Cross the stile to a fenced path. Continue past houses and a school on your left but turn right over a road bridge back to the river path. Turn left to retrace your steps to the car park.*

River Avon

3 *When you reach a public footpath signpost to Devizes Road, on your left, turn right to cross the Avon by a footbridge. Go ahead to a road. Turn left at Old Sarum View.*

P

1 *Start from Salisbury's main car park, which is signposted from Castle Street.*
Walk back to the river and walk away from the town centre with the river on your right. Continue under road and rail bridges, with the river still on your right. When you reach a children's playground on your left, bear away from the river.

2 *Turn right along the signposted footpath. This is the legal right of way. A popular unofficial alternative is to continue along the bank of the river, but although there are stiles over the fences, there may be muddy patches in wet weather.*

Salisbury

Walk 8
OLD WARDOUR CASTLE
4 miles (6.4 km) Easy

This is a walk with extensive views in one of the least spoilt parts of Wiltshire, close to the northern limit of Cranborne Chase. You can start from the car park at Old Wardour Castle. Alternatively, an excellent way to reach here is by train, on the scenic route between Salisbury and Yeovil. Alight at Tisbury, just as Jude and Sue Bridehead did in Hardy's *Jude the*

Obscure. A walk along the minor road south-west of Tisbury, going under the railway bridge and bearing right, brings you to point 7 on our walk. This is also the place to start if you come by bus (no. 26, Salisbury-Shaftesbury service). Like Jude and Sue, you are to walk past Wardour Castle, although this walk visits the ruined castle as well. As you enjoy the

view to the north, towards Fonthill, think of Sue and Jude walking across the 'open country, wide and high' to a station on another line, 'about seven miles off' to the north. This was most probably Boyton (now closed) on the Salisbury-Westbury line. A pleasant woodland path completes the circle back to Old Wardour Castle.

A Old Wardour Castle has a superb lakeside setting. Its romantic ruins and surrounding parkland were landscaped in the late 18th century. The castle's tall, hexagonal shape now stands in harmony with tall trees, while the Gothic-style banqueting house built beside the curtain wall has been recently restored. The castle is in the care of English Heritage and is open daily from April to September and on winter weekends. The site is indeed old, with King Alfred the Great probably having a royal manor here. He may have granted it to Wilton Abbey, as its nuns were the overlords of Wardour from at least Domesday Book to the 16th century. Sir Matthew Arundell purchased the property in 1570 and began to rebuild the castle in 1578. His son, Thomas Arundell, was raised to the peerage as Baron Arundell of Wardour by James I in 1605.

The Arundells were renowned for their Roman Catholicism, so it comes as no surprise to find Wardour the scene of bitter fighting in the Civil War. Sir Edward

Hungerford led 1300 Parliamentarian troops against the castle's garrison of 25 men, aided by a number of female servants, in April 1643. In the absence of her husband (in Oxford with the King), Lady Blanche Arundell led the castle's resistance until 8th May. Lord Arundell's grandchildren were captured and forced to receive a Puritan education in Essex. Having spitefully destroyed the orchards and fish-ponds, the Parliamentarians then held the castle with a garrison of cavalry and infantry under Edmund Ludlow. The Royalists were strong in Wiltshire, however, while Lord Arundell sought the return of his property. The situation dragged on until 18th March, 1644, when lack of food forced Ludlow to surrender. After the Restoration, the Arundells built a small house on the south side of the curtain wall and the castle was left as a ruin, to be surrounded by formal gardens in the 18th century.

B A new Wardour Castle was built to the Palladian design of

James Paine between 1768 and 1776. This is the place visited by Sue and Jude, as Hardy recorded: 'Tomorrow is our grand day, you know. Where shall we go?' 'I have leave from three till nine. Wherever we can get to and come back from in that time. Not ruins, Jude - I don't care for them.' 'Well Wardour Castle. And then we can do Fonthill if we like - all in the same afternoon.'

The fine art collection was dispersed after the death of the last Earl of Arundell in 1944. The family then sold the (new) castle to a religious order for conversion into a seminary. This caused the stripping out of the decorated ceilings and wall-panelling. Since 1960, the castle has housed a girl's school, but it is open on Mondays, Wednesdays, Fridays and Saturdays in the summer holidays.

0   1 mile
0   1 km

5 *Turn right along this road. When the road turns right, keep straight on along the private road, which is a public footpath.*

6 *Go ahead along the minor road, which joins your path from the left.*

7 *Turn right along the lane and continue along it for half a mile (0.8 km).*

8 *Bear left up a track to 'Fox Farm'. The forest is on your right, while there are extensive views across Nadder valley on your left. Ignore a track on your right, just before a house, and continue through conifer plantations.*

9 *Immediately after a track joins yours from the left, turn right. Go straight across a track to follow a fenced path between two fields. Bear right with this path through woodland (ignore a path coming from your right). Continue under an arch to walk with a fence on your left. Emerge from the wood back at the car park, with the castle on your left.*

1 *Start from the car park at Old Wardour Castle. This is signposted 2 miles (3.2 km) south-west of Tisbury and 1.5 miles (2.4 km) north of the A30 road between Wilton and Shaftesbury.*
Walk along the track with the castle on your left and the lake on your right.

2 *This track soon bends right, with trees across the field on your left.*

4 *Go through a gate ahead to follow the crescent driveway past Cranborne Chase school on your left. Follow the driveway to the road.*

3 *Fork right along the fenced track. When this track bends right to farm buildings, keep straight on with the hedge on your right.*

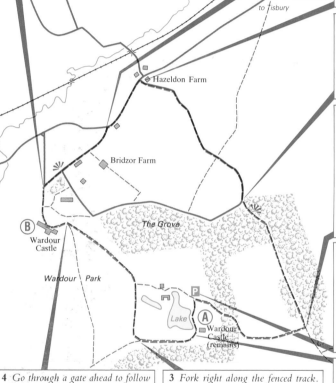

Walk 9

JACK THE TREACLE EATER

3.5 miles (5.6 km) Moderate

0   1 mile
0   1 km

This is a varied, interesting walk on the edge of Yeovil. It passes through parkland laid out in an informal style and includes a woodland walk. Yeovil Junction Station is about half way round the walk, so British Rail travellers should join the circle at point 7.

The route is clear and waymarked with yellow arrows on wooden posts. This was an initiative of the South Somerset District Council.

2 Cross a bridge, turn left and cross a second bridge to follow the path uphill, bearing left to follow a level path (ignoring turnings downhill and uphill) until you reach a little waterfall.

3 Ford the stream above the waterfall on your left and continue across railings (in the broken kissing-gate). Veer right uphill to a kissing-gate at the top. Go ahead with the hedge on your left.

4 Go through a kissing-gate, cross a road and continue over a stile signposted 'Barwick'. Pause to see the Fish Tower on your left. Go ahead across this field to a waymarked stile beside a gate. Bear left to reach a stile giving access to the drive of Barwick House. Turn left, passing a lake on your right.

5 Turn left when you reach a road, pausing to notice Jack the Treacle Eater's arch in the parkland on your left. After 300 yards (270 m), turn right down a fenced path waymarked 'Yeovil Junction'. Pass a bungalow on your left and look for a wooden footbridge to cross the stream ahead on your right.

6 Go over the stile above the footbridge and cross a field to another stile. Turn left to follow the path past the backs of houses to a road. Do not go under the railway bridge on your right, but follow the lane towards Yeovil Junction Station.

1 Park your car at the Old Station car park at the south of Yeovil town centre.
Start walking along the gravel path at the right of the car park. Fork right to pass a play area on your left.

9 Follow the path through the woods. When you reach a stile, walk down an open field, bearing left to a stile and bridge to the car park.

8 Turn right along the road. Pass a road turning on your left, then 300 yards (270 m) later, bear left up a track signposted 'Round House'. Look carefully for a path through the trees on your right after about 60 yards (55 m), waymarked 'Yeovil Old Station'.

7 Turn left through a gate before the station to follow a track above a river on your left. Cross the river by a concrete bridge and bear right across a field to rails in a gap in the hedge ahead.

A Ninesprings were landscaped in the 18th-century by the owners of Aldon House. Little waterfalls drop down a tiny valley.

B The Fish Tower is one of the 18th century follies of Barwick Park. George Messiter supposedly built them to provide work for unemployed glove-makers.

C This folly, an archway, is named after one of Messiter's young workmen who ate treacle to sustain him on several trips to London.

20

Walk 10
STURMINSTER NEWTON
2 miles (3.2 km) Easy

0   1 mile
0   1 km

Sturminster Newton was Thomas Hardy's Stourcastle. The town is tucked into a bend of the River Stour and takes its name from its church (minster) on this river. The locals know it as Stur. It is the gateway to the Vale of Blackmore, a wide clay vale watered by deep springs in a narrow band of greensand soil at the foot of the steep chalk. The place has retained the atmosphere of a small market town of Hardy's Wessex. The novelist lived here from July 1876 to March 1878, describing them as the happiest two years of his married life with Emma. Hardy wrote *The Return of the Native* here, plus several poems.

2 Go through the waymarked gate in the corner of the field, with Hardy's Riverside Villa on your right. Turn right to walk down to where a stile on your right indicates a cross-path. Turn left to cross the river by a footbridge (Colber Bridge).

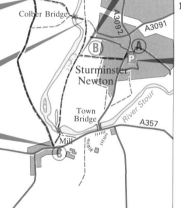

4 Turn left along a lane for half a mile (0.8 km). Just after Mill Cottage, turn left over a waymarked stile. Walk down to the mill.

3 Follow the yellow arrow to a stile beside a gate in the hedge ahead. Cross this stile and walk with a hedge on your left to a stile beside another gate.

5 Cross the river by the footbridges and follow the path through the waymarked gate. The path rises to reach another waymarked gate. Go through to reach Riverside Villa. Turn right to retrace your steps to the start.

1 Start from the octagonal base of the old Market Cross in the centre of Sturminster Newton. This is on the B3092 just across the bridge over the River Stour off the A357 about 9 miles (14.5 km) northwest of Blandford Forum. There are several signposted car parks, but the one opposite the National Westminster Bank is most convenient. A small fee allows you to park for 2 hours, which should be ample time for this short walk.

From the Market Cross, walk past the White Hart Inn on your right and turn right down Ricketts Lane. Pass the recreation ground on your left.

A The octagonal base and four steps of Sturminster Newton's 15th-century market cross can still be seen in the attractive square. The weekly cattle auction has outgrown this venue since Hardy's day and now takes place on the north side of town. The town itself is an agreeable jumble of architectural styles, with peaceful backlanes. Hardy described the girls dancing near the Market Cross on Coronation Day, 28th June, 1877. He drew upon this memory when writing of girls dancing in *Tess of the d'Urbervilles*. The town also had its own poet, William Barnes, who befriended Hardy.

B Hardy brought his wife, Emma, to Riverside Villa in July 1876. This was one of a semi-detached pair of houses overlooking the River Stour. One of these houses now bears an engraved slate plaque to commemorate their two-year tenancy, but it is probably attached to the wrong one. Hardy often walked across Colber Bridge, which was erected in 1841.

One of his poems was entitled *On Sturminster Footbridge*. Hardy remarked on the river's 'fishy smell from the numerous eels and other fish beneath'. Hardy indulged his love of rowing on the Stour, while his house enjoyed famous sunsets. When he returned here in 1916, after Emma's death, Hardy described Riverside Villa as her 'musical box'.

C In his poem *The Musical Box*, Hardy wrote of 'Stourside Mill, where broad/Stream-lilies throng'.

MELBURY BEACON

5 miles (8 km) Moderate

Melbury Beacon, which has an old Iron Age earthwork around its summit, provides some of the finest views in Dorset. Passengers from the X13 (Shaftesbury–Bournemouth) bus can start at Compton Abbas.

7 *Turn right through a gate beside a signpost to follow a track which gradually climbs beside a hedge and fence on your right to a gate. The track soon bends left uphill. Go straight up, through a second gate, to cross a stile to the Ordnance Survey trig. point at the summit of Melbury Hill. This is the site of the old beacon.*

6 *Continue along the lane, which bends to the left and reaches the A350 after 600 yards (549 m).* **Take great care** *as you turn right along this main road for 250 yards (229 m) past Apple Lynchet and Whitehall Cottage.*

5 *Fork right and then follow the lane around a sharp left bend to turn right towards East Compton. Visit the remains of St Mary's church, with its old Cross, on your left.*

4 *Go through a small gate in the corner of the field to follow an enclosed path which bears left to a lane in the village of Compton Abbas. Turn right along this lane.*

3 *Go through a gate near the foot of the hill and walk along the left-hand edge of the field to the hedge ahead. Turn right to walk with the hedge on your left.*

8 *Continue across a stile and turn right, with Shaftesbury away on your left. Follow the fence on your right and walk down to a stile beside a gate ahead. Cross the next field to a gap in the fence on your left and descend towards the village of Melbury Abbas.*

2 *Cross an old dyke and continue past a stile in the fence on your left. When you reach the end of the trees on your left, veer right downhill, passing an old parish boundary stone.*

9 *Turn right along the footpath at the bottom to walk through trees to a gate which leads to the road. Turn right up Spread Eagle Hill back to the car park.* **Although this is a minor road, beware of traffic,** *especially farm lorries.*

Melbury Beacon

Compton Down

East Compton

Compton Abbas

Fontmell Down

A350

1 *Start from the car park near the summit of Spread Eagle Hill on a minor road 2 miles (3.2 km) south of Shaftesbury, past the village of Melbury Abbas.*
The car park is on your right as you go south, and a stile from it invites you onto National Trust land at Fontmell Down. Go ahead, with a fence on your left.

A Fontmell Down is rich in butterflies and chalkland flora. This part is owned by the National Trust.

B The 15th-century church of St Mary's in East Compton was demolished in 1867. Notice the steps of the old cross in the churchyard.

C Melbury Beacon is 862 feet (263 m) high and affords magnificent views north to Shaftesbury and east over Cranborne Chase.

Walk 12
HOD HILL
3 miles (4.8 km) Moderate

Hod Hill is one of several hill forts guarding the valley of the River Stour. Its name is of some significance to ley-hunters and followers of Alfred Waltkins' old straight tracks. Hod recalls the box carried on the shoulder with the aid of a rod - the staff of the original surveyors of these ancient earthworks. These unploughed slopes are rich in flora and fauna; the riverside walk is a special treat.

3 *Bear right with the track through trees to a road. Turn right just before the road to climb up to a gate signposted 'Hod Hill'. Walk uphill with the trees on your right.*

4 *Cross the stile beside a gate ahead to enter the hill fort at the corner used by the Romans. Explore all of the fort as you make for the bottom left-hand corner.*

5 *Descend along the hedged track back to Stourpaine, walking beside the River Iwerne at the foot of the hill. Turn right along Manor Road and retrace your steps to your car, or the bus stop, from the crossroads.*

2 *Turn right up Hod Drive, the track signposted 'Bridleway to Hanford'. Pass beneath Hod Hill on your right and beside the River Stour on your left.*

1 *Start from the White Horse pub on the A350 in Stourpaine, 2 miles (3.2 km) north-west of Blandford Forum. Park beside the White Horse or in the village. The X13 and 139 buses stop here.*
Turn left from the White Horse and left again down South Holme. Go ahead across Manor Road to Havelins, the road opposite, which crosses the River Iwerne.

Leigh Wood

Hod Hill Fort

River Stour

Hod Drive

River Iwerne

A350

Stourpaine

Church

P

A The western side of Hod Hill, overlooking the Stour valley, is the steepest side, requiring only a low bank to defend its summit. It is a site of special scientific interest and the footpath at its base is considered to be one of the prettiest paths in Dorset. Six species of orchids survive here - pyramidal, fragrant, frog, bee, twayblade and common spotted. Horseshoe vetch, devil's bit scabious, clustered bellflower and autumn gentian are also here, while Hod Hill's blackberry bushes provide a habitat for the great green bush cricket. The bottom path is through ash-wood with hart's tongue ferns, with beech and London plane trees near the end. Bird-nest orchids may even be seen.

B When the Romans captured the Iron Age hill fort of Hod Hill in either AD 43 or 44, Vespasian's Second Legion Augusta built its own fort in the north-western corner and highest part of the British camp. It was garrisoned by 600 legionary infantry and an auxiliary cavalry unit of 250 men and their horses.

C Hod Hill is one of the largest of the Dorset hill forts, with an internal area of 54 acres (21.9 ha). It was developed over the whole of the Iron Age, with ditches and ramparts being added to make it impregnable until the Romans brought their lethal ballista machine to it on a movable siege-tower and rained ballista bolts on the Durotrigic chieftain's hut. Slight depressions in the ground indicate other British huts set alight by Roman fire arrows.

Walk 13
BOKERLEY DYKE
4 miles (6.4 km) Moderate

This is a walk in superb countryside full of historical interest. It is based on Pentridge, which was renamed 'Trantridge' by Hardy. Tess was a farm worker here, while Alec d'Urberville lived in Trantridge with his widowed mother. Tess walked the tracks from here to Chaseborough (Cranborne) for some Saturday night fun at the fair. General Augustus Pitt-Rivers, who excavated Bokerley Dyke, was a friend of Hardy.

A Where the path reaches the road, it crosses the course of the Dorset Cursus. This is a Neolithic (New Stone Age) earthwork running north-east from near Blandford Forum and is one of the largest prehistoric monuments in Britain. It consists of two parallel banks about 90 yards (82 m) apart and seems to have been a forerunner of the stone avenues such as those at Avebury. The number of barrows in this area has led to the suggestion that the Cursus could have been a processional way to them. Unfortunately, however, there is nothing to be seen here now as all trace of the Cursus has been ploughed out at this end. The best place to see this mysterious monument, which runs for 7 miles (11.2 km) across Cranborne Chase, is near Wyke Down, about 2 miles (3.2 km) south-west of Pentridge. Turn off the A354 along the B3081 for half a mile (0.8 km), where it crosses Ackling Dyke, the old Roman road. There is a right of way along this Roman road. Walk south along it for 1 mile (1.6 km) to where it crosses a well-preserved section of the Cursus.

B Notice a Neolithic long barrow in the field on your right. This is one of several long and round barrows in this area.

C Bokerley Dyke, or Ditch, is an impressive earthwork dividing the modern counties of Dorset, to the south, and Hampshire, to the north. It is not the result of any county boundary changes in 1974, however, as it dates from more warlike days when Britons clashed with Saxons at the end of the Roman occupation. Its origin is open to speculation because of the civil disturbances at this time. The Dyke has been accurately dated, however, with several stages of construction having been identified. Pitt-Rivers made his most celebrated excavation here between 1888 and 1891. He was able to show how the 4 mile (6.4 km) long Dyke plugged a gap beside the Roman road, Ackling Dyke, which connected Badbury Rings and Old Sarum. Its flanks were covered by forest. Initially, about AD 360, the road passed by the barrier. The Dyke was then extended across the road, blocking it. This may have been in 367 (coins of Valens, who was emperor from 364 to 378, were found). The Roman road was then re-opened, only to be blocked for good in about 395 (a coin of Honorius, dating from 393, was found). The Dyke's Hampshire side is more impressive and would have faced the Saxons. Its defenders on the Dorset side would have been the cultured Durotriges tribe. The Saxons were held at bay for about 150 years, well into the 6th century and long enough for Dorset to retain a Celtic character. Martin Down, on the Hampshire side of the Dyke, is a National Nature Reserve. Its unploughed sheep pasture supports chalkland butterflies, such as the silver-spotted skipper and the adonis blue. You may even see a ground nesting stone curlew, but remember that it is an offence to deliberately approach or disturb this bird during the nesting season.

D The less impressive earthwork leading off at a right angle from Bokerley Dyke is known as Grim's Ditch. It may date from the Bronze Age.

E Penbury Knowle is crowned by a simple single ditch Iron Age hill fort.

F The influence of Bokerley Dyke may have led to Pentridge church being dedicated to the Celtic saint Rumbold. Look for a memorial on the north wall of the nave to the great-great-grandfather of the poet Robert Browning, also known as Robert Browning, who died in 1746.

0   1 mile

0   1 km

3 *Continue ahead, ignoring a track which joins yours from the right. Follow the downland path to the great earthwork of Bokerley Dyke. This marks the boundary between Dorset and Hampshire. Pass the Nature Reserve notice and turn right to walk on the Hampshire side of the Dyke. There are fine views over Hampshire and Wiltshire on your left, while the Dyke is on your right.*

4 *Turn right along the chalk track which cuts through the Dyke by the Nature Reserve board. After 100 yards (90 m) turn sharp right along the track waymarked with blue arrows. Turn left off this after another 100 yards (90 m) through a small gate waymarked with blue arrows. Walk with a fence on your right through trees to emerge overlooking the Dyke, going away on your right. Continue with the fence on your right until you reach the corner of a field.*

2 *Turn left along the road until it turns left. Turn right at this corner to follow a green lane. Keep right when you reach a fork.*

Cursus

Ⓒ

Ⓑ

Ⓓ

Bokerley Dyke

Bokerley Down

A354

Ⓐ

Ⓕ

Pentridge

Dorset

Pentridge Down

Penbury Knoll

Ⓔ

1 *Park your car in the village of Pentridge and start the walk from the church. Pentridge is on the left as you travel along the A354 from Salisbury to Blandford Forum. Buses (nos. 184 and 185) from these places stop where the lane for Pentridge leaves the main road.*
With the church behind you, cross the village green to go through a small gate ahead. Continue with the hedge on your left to a gate which gives access to the road.

6 *Turn right when you reach the woody summit of Penbury Knoll, where the ramparts of an old camp can be traced. Walk downhill towards the steeple of Pentridge church. Look for a stile in the bottom left-hand corner of the field and cross it to go down a fenced path. Go ahead over another stile to bear right down to a road. Turn right along the road, then turn left up the lane to St Rumbold's Church.*

5 *The right of way bears left across this field to a prominent group of ash trees. You may find this path ploughed and obstructed by crops, although the farmer will also have probably left a clear headland path around the edge of the field which you should follow to the trees. Go through the gate behind the trees to walk with the hedge and views over the New Forest on your left.*

25

Walk 14
BREAMORE MIZMAZE
5 miles (8 km) Easy

This is a peaceful walk along clear tracks across farmland and through woodland. The importance of breeding race-horses to the local economy is evident and gives this rural scene a special character. Its chief asset is a rare maze hidden in the woods – a perfect setting. The nearby Breamore House could be Hardy's 'Arrowthorne Lodge' in his novel *The Hand of Ethelberta*. If you rely on public transport, start the walk at Breamore House. This is signposted from Breamore, which is on the route of the X3 bus between Poole and Salisbury. This will add an extra mile (1.6 km) to the walk.

A If it weren't for the trees that have overgrown its ditch beside this bridleway, you would have a fine view of Whitsbury Iron Age camp. It is surrounded by a triple circle of great banks with two deep ditches in between them. A circular timber house of 25 feet (7.5 m) diameter was excavated inside it in 1960, and Iron Age pottery found. The camp formed a link in the defensive chain which held up the Saxon advance into this area of Britain until the late 6th century. The Romans sank a 300 feet (90 m) well near the camp's western entrance. Finds of 2nd-century coins suggest that a Romano-British village existed at Whitsbury. Whitsbury probably derived its name from the colour of it chalky soil. Alfred Watkins, however, whose *Old Straight Track* was published in 1925, identified 'white' names with ancient salt tracks.

B Breamore Mizmaze is ideally situated in a woodland clearing. This is a large maze with a diameter of 87 feet (26.5 m) and a low mound about 6 inches (0.15 m) high and 18 feet (5.4 m) in diameter at its centre. The Mizmaze is a labyrinth cut into the turf whose exact purpose and date of construction are unknown. The Labyrinth at Knossos, in Crete, was of a similar design. It has no false paths to lead you astray, just a single laborious route to the centre. A pattern soon emerges, with symmetry obviously important. The 'turn maze' could have been trodden as a significant ritual as long ago as the Bronze Age (1500 B.C.). Mazes, or 'Troy towns' (a name which may be a clue to their origin) used to be fairly common, but only eight in the whole of Britain seem to have survived. Cromwell's puritan fanatics were responsible for destroying many of them.

C Breamore House is a fine Elizabethan Manor House. It is open to the public every afternoon from April to September, except Mondays and Fridays. It contains a fine collection of paintings and furniture.

D You can also visit the Countryside and Carriage Museum, with its smithy and old steam engines.

E Upper Street contains some very well-preserved thatched cottages.

F St Leonard's Church, Whitsbury, dates from at least the 12th century, although the present building is mostly 19th century. William Hill restored and refurnished the church in 1963, emphasising the village's links with the world of horse racing. St Leonard is the patron saint of prisoners.

0   1 mile
0   1 km

3 At the bottom of the hill, go ahead across a track to go over a stile beside a gate. Keep straight on with the hedge on your right to reach woodland. Continue over cross-tracks to walk out of the wood to a stile beside a gate.

2 Do not turn right at the sign to Whitsbury Manor Stud, but do turn right 30 yards (27 m) later at the signposted bridleway, where the road bends left. Follow this surfaced track, with the manor house and its stables on your right. Bend right behind the stables with this track before forking left along a signposted bridleway.

4 Turn right along this track. Look for a sign on the edge of the woods on your right. This will point out the way to the Mizmaze, which is hidden in the woods. Bear right to see it. Return to the track and bear left between two hedges. Fork right to follow the path through woodland.

5 Pass Breamore House on your left. Follow the driveway to a gateway guarded by stone lions. Turn right, passing the Countryside and Carriage Museum on your left. When you reach a corner of a road, turn right. Pass the thatched cottages of Upper Street and turn right at a grassy triangle. This road leads to a hedged track.

South Charford Drove

Mizmaze
Ⓑ

Giant's
Grave

Ⓐ
Fort

Breamore   Wood

Ⓒ
Breamore
House

Ⓕ Church

Whitsbury

Church

Ⓟ

Breamore Ⓓ

Ⓔ

1 Start from the village of Whitsbury, which is on a minor road 4 miles (6.4 km) north-west of Fordingbridge. Park your car in the village, perhaps near the Cartwheel Inn.
Walk up the main street, away from Fordingbridge towards Whitsbury manor house and stud farm.

7 When this track starts to bend right, turn left towards a farm. Go ahead through the farmyard and walk up a tree-lined track to woods. Turn right at the far side of these woods to a house with lamp posts. Turn left along the fenced track. At its end, bear left, then right, to reach Whitsbury Church. Go through the gate opposite the church door to follow a fenced path back to the village of Whitsbury.

6 Ignore a left fork and go ahead to a stile beside a gate. Continue with the hedge on your left to a gate. Turn right along a track.

Walk 15

EVERSHOT

5 miles (8 km) Easy, but sometimes muddy

This is a varied walk through scenery described by Hardy in *The Woodlanders*. It starts at Evershot which, at an altitude of 700 feet (180 m), is the second highest village in Dorset. It descends to follow muddy green lanes to Melbury Osmond, the home of Hardy's mother. The walk then follows well-surfaced estate driveways past Melbury House and through its deer-park.

A The Acorn Inn was renamed the 'Sow and Acorn' in *Tess of the D'Urbervilles*. Tess avoided it, but Tupcombe, Squire Dornell's man, sat in its inglenook in the hope of hearing news of Betty. Here, too, Philip Hall collected Sally's dress from the carrier in *Interlopers at the Knap*.

B 'Tess' Cottage' is across Back Lane from the church. This is where Tess had breakfast on her way to 'Emminster' (Beaminster) to see Angel's parents. Evershot was renamed 'Evershead' by Hardy. Its real name is derived from the Anglo-Saxon for 'wild boar thicket'. St Osmond's church was rebuilt in the 19th century but has a Norman font. The poet George Crabbe was rector here from 1783 to 1787.

C St John's Well is on your right about 200 yards (180 m) from the church down Back Lane. This is the source of the River Frome, which flows through Dorset to reach the sea at Poole harbour. It was near here that Tess discovered Alec d'Urberville ranting in a barn (now demolished).

D The mixed deciduous woodland is like that in which Giles Winterborne made his home in a 'one-chimney hut' that so contrasted with nearby Melbury House. Giles had resorted to a deserted charcoal burner's cottage after being evicted from his home. He was unable to renew his lease when it reverted to the landowner after the expiration of a given number of generations. This gloomy image of blighted crops and stunted growth pervades *The Woodlanders*. Such is the natural world, but Hardy also extols Nature, with evocative forest scenes. It is to here that Grace Melbury comes, escaping from her faithless husband and seeking Giles' help. She finds 'a square cot of one storey only, sloping up on all sides to a chimney in the midst .... the room within was kitchen, parlour and bedchamber all in one; the natural sandstone floor was worn into hills and dales by long treading, so that none of the furniture stood level, and the table slanted like a desk.'

E Hardy's parents' families had once owned land around Melbury Osmond so it is natural to locate *The Woodlanders*, with its theme of lost status due to loss of property, here. Melbury Osmond was, indeed, the original for Hardy's 'Great Hintock'. Not wishing to offend the Earl of Ilchester, who lived in Melbury House, Hardy tried to move the location further east in the novel's second edition. Melbury Osmond now became 'King's Hintock'. The last scene of *The Woodlanders* is still definitely set in Melbury Osmond, however, with Marty in the moonlight beside Giles' grave in 'Great Hintock' churchyard. This church was where Hardy's parents, Thomas Hardy (senior) and Jemima Hand, were married on 22nd December, 1839. Hardy's mother used to live in the thatched cottage on the north side of the church.

F Melbury House was originally Hardy's 'Hintock House' but it became 'King's Hintock Court' in the second edition of *The Woodlanders*. In reality it is a manor house built by Sir Giles Strangways shortly before 1540. It is now a stud farm for race-horses.

G Melbury Park was Hardy's 'King's Hintock Park' and your route is along the tree-lined driveway that the enigmatic stranger used in *The Duke's Reappearance*. Look out for three types of deer here - red, fallow and Japanese sika. The private drive is a public path.

0   1 mile
0   1 km

8 Continue along the hedged track, which soon bears left to cross a stream and then bear right. Go under an archway before bearing left to emerge between two thatched cottages at the side of a road.

9 Turn right along this road to reach Melbury Osmond and its church. Retrace your steps and continue to enter the parkland of Melbury House. Go ahead along the driveway that is also the public path. Keep straight on towards Melbury House.

7 Walk with the fence on your right past a waymark post. At the end of the field, turn right through a small gate and turn left immediately along a track. Continue through a gate to meet a road as it bends towards a house on your left. Go straight across this road to the muddy track opposite. Continue through a gate at the end of this hedged track and cross a corner of a field to a small gate ahead.

10 Just before Melbury House, turn right with the driveway. Follow it as it bends left and uphill through a deer park. Eventually the drive descends to the road at the grassy triangle where you started.

6 Just after passing a thatched boathouse on your right, go ahead through a gate and turn right, off the main tracks. Bear left through a gate before a bridge across a stream and a gate after it.

5 Bear left, passing deciduous woodland on your right. When you have a fenced field on your left, look for glimpses of Lucerne Lake through the trees on your right.

4 Fork right along an uphill track. Continue through trees and past a water tower on your left at the top of the hill. Walk down to the bottom of the hill, passing conifer trees on your left and a conifer plantation between two fields on your right.

3 Turn left along the road and fork left towards Melbury House.

1 Start from the grassy triangle at the bottom of the hill in the east end of Evershot. This is both the bus stop (Comfy Lux nos 211 and 212 between Dorchester, Sherborne and Yeovil) and roadside parking (but keep the driveway to Melbury House clear). Evershot is at a junction of minor roads 1.5 miles (2.4 km) west of the A37 where it crosses the Bristol to Weymouth railway line at Holywell.
Walk away from the driveway to Melbury House, passing Back Lane on your right and following the main road as it bends right into Fore Street, passing Summer Lane on your left.

2 Turn right along Back Lane, between Tess' Cottage and St Osmond's church. Follow Back Lane as it bends right to meet the road near your start.

Walk 16

UP SYDLING

4 miles (6.4 km) Moderate

0 _____ 1 mile
0 _____ 1 km

This walk crosses attractive, open land in an isolated area of high, dry chalkland where water had to be collected in dew ponds. These were made in ancient times by using clay to form an artificial pond to be filled by atmospheric condensation. There are extensive views looking north towards Yeovil.

7 Go ahead along a hedged path in the corner of this field. Emerge at the corner of a road where you turn left immediately through a gate to follow a track past barns on your left and with a tall hedge on your right. Pass a fenced field on your left. Ignore two tracks which branch off on your left and keep beside the hedge on your right. Bear right when the hedge turns right to reach the A37 at the lay-by where you started this walk.

1 Park your car in a lay-by on the A37 road between Dorchester and Yeovil about 500 yards (450 m) south of the Clay Pigeon Restaurant (and nearly 2 miles (3.2 km) north of the turn-offs to Sydling St Nicholas). This is just before a 'Campsite 400 yards' roadsign, as you come from Dorchester. The 212 bus route between Yeovil and Dorchester passes here.
A waymark post with a blue arrow stands by the field entrance on your left as you stand in the lay-by with the 'Campsite' sign at your back. DO NOT set out along this path. WALK SOUTH along the roadside verge for 700 yards (630 m) to the next gateway on your left, which also has a waymark post with a blue arrow.

6 Turn only half-right to walk across to the far corner of the field where there is a dew pond. Bear left through a gate to the left of the pond and go ahead to a road. Turn left along the road. Ignore tracks on your left and a road going downhill on your right. About 50 yards (45 m) after this road, however, bear left to follow the hedge on your left.

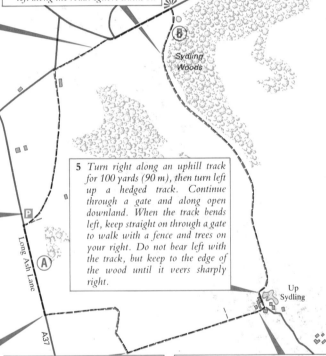

5 Turn right along an uphill track for 100 yards (90 m), then turn left up a hedged track. Continue through a gate and along open downland. When the track bends left, keep straight on through a gate to walk with a fence and trees on your right. Do not bear left with the track, but keep to the edge of the wood until it veers sharply right.

2 Turn left through the gate to walk with the hedge on your left. Go on through a gate and walk downhill. Turn right near the bottom of this field. Descend to a gate ahead and walk with a hedge on your left.

3 Turn left through a gate to walk with a hedge on your right. The hedge will switch to your left but continue ahead to the end of this field.

4 Turn left and immediately right to follow a hedged track. Pass farm buildings on your left and turn left past a lake on your right.

A This is the Long Ash Lane that Hardy describes as ill-kept in Inter-lopers at the Knap and The Grave by the Handpost.

B This is a large dew pond at a height of 780 feet (234 m).

Walk 17
PLUSH
4.5 miles (7.2 km) Moderate

0   1 mile

0   1 km

The chalk hills form an amphitheatre around Plush, making this a quiet, remote place. Parking spaces are not specifically provided, but the lack of through traffic makes considerate roadside parking possible near the old inn at Folly. The views are superb, especially of Blackmoor Vale.

6 Go ahead along the downland path for half a mile (0.8 km). Turn right to walk with the hedge on your left. Veer right to a square earthwork and continue past a dew pond to a gate in the corner. Bear right to a sign which points to Folly. Bear left through a gate and continue with a hedge on your left to return to Folly.

1 Park at the roadside north of Folly, which is between Piddletrenthide and Mappowder, about 10 miles (16 km) north-west of Dorchester. Walk eastwards along the track which crosses the road, passing a farmhouse on your right.

2 Fork right up a greener track to a gate. Bear right to the top of the down. Pass trees on your left and bear right beside the fence on your left, behind which is an Ordnance Survey pillar. Go ahead through a gate in the corner of the field, turn left through a small gate and immediately turn right.

Church Hill

Ball Hill

Folly

Cross Dyke

Cross Dyke

Cross Dyke

Cross Dyke

Higher Hill

▲ 244

Plush

5 Turn right up the gated bridleway signposted 'Alton Pancras 1¼'. Bear right through trees and go uphill beside a hedge on your right. Continue through a gate and past trees on your right to go through another gate.

4 Go through a small gate to descend to the bottom right-hand corner of this field. Go through a gate and turn left along the road through Plush.

3 Walk with the fence on your right to a gate on your right near a concrete reservoir. Turn right to follow the path down to a bar stile. Cross it and veer slightly right downhill.

A This pillar is a 'trig.' point or triangulation station set up by the Ordnance Survey.

B Plush is the model for Hardy's village of 'Flintcombe-Ash' in *Tess of the d'Urbervilles*.

C Hardy's imaginary 'Flintcombe-Ash Farm' was situated on the slopes of Church Hill. Old Celtic fields still mark this hill.

D This square enclosure has not been dated.

Walk 18
DOGBURY HILL
5.5 miles (8.8 km) Moderate

| 0 | | | 1 mile |
| 0 | | 1 km | |

This is a splendid route for views, with your path reaching a height of 870 feet (265 m). Good, clear tracks are followed, making this a walk suitable for all (although there may be large puddles after wet weather). Hardy moved the location of *The Woodlanders* here after its first edition and enough belts of woodland have survived to make this setting authentic.

1 *Park at a lay-by on the A352 road north of Minterne Magna. As you come from Dorchester, which is 10 miles (16 km) to the south, the lay-by is on your right just after a converted school-house.*

Go through the gate between the school-house and the lay-by and walk ahead to a second gate which is waymarked with blue arrows. Bear slightly left across the field to a stile in the top fence. Cross a narrow field to a gate ahead.

2 *Turn right, along the fenced track that is an old ridgeway. After passing through woodland on Dogbury Hill, the path affords splendid views both to the left (over North Dorset and Somerset) and to the right (overlooking Minterne House and the upper Cerne valley). Pass a plantation of trees on your right.*

4 *Go ahead at the cross-tracks, pass a farmyard on your right and a dovecot and the stump of Minterne Parva's old medieval cross on your left. Walk down the lane to the A352.*

5 *Turn left along the A352 for 200 yards (180 m), then turn right up the lane to Upper Cerne.*

3 *Just after the end of the fencing on your right and just before the ridge-way bends left, turn right through a gate to follow a grassy track which soon bears left downhill. Emerge from the woodland along a sunken green track which descends to a second gate. Continue along a hedged track which gradually bears right.*

0   1 mile
0   1 km

9 *Turn right along this minor road until you reach a corner where the road bends sharply right.*

11 *Turn right when you reach another minor road. Follow it until its junction with the A352 at* Dogbury Gate, where you turn right to very carefully walk back to your car at the lay-by on your left.

A352

High Stoy

D

Dogbury Gate

E

P

Telegraph Hill

Dogbury Hill

10 *Turn left off the road at this corner to follow a hedged, grassy track. Bear right with this track down through woodland. Continue along the bottom edge of this wood. Across the hedge on your left you can catch a glimpse of Somerset.*

Minterne Magna

A

Little Minterne Hill

8 *Follow the distinct path through the wood and continue across a narrow field to a roadside waymark post.*

7 *Go to the right of the barn and walk with the hedge on your left. When this track turns left, go straight ahead across a field towards woodland.*

Minterne Parva

B

6 *Turn right at the bus shelter to walk with a stream on your right. Continue past the Great Pond, which can be glimpsed through the trees on your left. This lane deteriorates to a rough track as it climbs. Ignore a track on your left and go ahead to a metal barn.*

Up Cerne

C

A352

A Minterne Magna replaced Melbury Osmond as Hardy's 'Great Hintock'.

B Minterne Parva is a tiny hamlet with an old dovecote.

C Upper Cerne's manor house dates from the 16th century.

D High Stoy was one of Hardy's favourite viewpoints and was climbed by the four friends in the poem *Under High Stoy Hill*.

E Dogbury Gate's name refers to the old turnpike gate that used to stand here. Hardy's poem *Life and Death at Sunrise* is set here.

CERNE ABBAS
3.5 miles (5.6 km) Moderate

Cerne Abbas is most famous for its male nude giant carved into the chalk of the nearby hillside, best seen from the lay-by at the start of this walk. Access to the giant is not officially allowed now, but your route passes under his feet. If you do see anybody venturing closer to the figure known locally as 'His Mightiness', she (for it is more relevant to women) is probably either about to get married or is hoping to become pregnant. The giant is of ancient pagan origin and its survival seems incredible, especially as it had Christian monks living at its feet for centuries. Hardy noted the old belief that a living giant who ate human flesh and terrorised the neighbourhood was captured and killed here and that the outline of his huge body was carved in the chalk of the hillside where he lay. Mrs Cantle transferred the tale to Napoleon in *The Dynasts*, saying:

'I can tell you a word or two on't. It is about his victuals. They say that he lives upon human flesh, and has rashers of baby every morning for breakfast – for all the world like the Cernal Giant in old ancient times!' Cerne Abbas was Hardy's 'Abbot's Cernel', referring to its old abbey. The once flourishing town was in decline when Hardy wrote but its outstanding beauty has since attracted many to retire here.

A The Cerne giant is 180 feet (55 m) high and brandishes a 120 feet (36 m) club. It has survived the centuries by being regularly scoured and tended by the locals, who regard it as safeguarding the fertility of their land. The giant is now in the care of the National Trust.

It survived the Victorian period intact under the protection of the pioneering archaeologist, General Pitt-Rivers. It is obviously connected with fertility. Making love on the grass of the giant's phallus is a traditional cure for barrenness. Barren women come to just sit on the tip of the phallus, while women about to get married come to walk around the whole figure to ensure a happy marriage. The giant's association with fertility is strengthened by its link with Beltane, May-Day. The eve of Beltane was the time for many to lose their virginity in the woods. A sightline taken vertically up the middle of the phallus on May Day would point directly at the rising sun as it came over the down.

The name Cerne may refer to Cernunnos, the Celtic lord of the wild beasts and a giant who wielded a club. The Giant was most probably adopted by the Romans when Commodus was emperor (180 – 93 BC). Commodus claimed to be the incarnation of Hercules and assumed the title of Hercules Romanus. Evidence of a lion's skin draped over the giant's left arm (now overgrown) supports this theory.

B The ancient earthwork above the giant's outstretched arm is the Trendle or Frying Pan. A flat platform may have had a ceremonial purpose. The Cerne Abbas village May Pole might have stood here. Prisoners may have been kept in the Trendle to await sacrifice in the Beltane fire, perhaps in a wickerwork giant (called a 'kolosson' by the Romans).

C The parish church of St Mary.

D St Augustine's Well: St Augustine is said to have put his staff into the ground and out flowed water. He named the place Cernel from the Latin 'Cerno' (I see) and Hel (the giant?). Women drink here in the hope of becoming pregnant while a wishing stone has a St Catherine's Wheel carved on it for women to pray for a husband. A ley line passes through this stone and up to the Trendle.

E The old abbey church stood here. A 9th-century monastery was refounded on Benedictine lines in 987 and dissolved by Henry VIII in 1539.

F The sumptuous porch to the now vanished Abbot's Lodging stands in the grounds of Abbey Farm. The secretly-married

0   1 mile

0   1 km

3 Ignore a stile on your left but go ahead across a stile and bear left to pass under the feet of the giant on your right. Continue parallel with the hedge on your left. Veer right uphill when you reach a patch of woodland and a cattle trough on your left.

1 Park your car in the 'Giant View' lay-by off the A352 north of Cerne Abbas. This is 8 miles (12.8 km) north of Dorchester. Cerne Abbas is served by buses (nos 6, 116 & 203) from Dorchester and Sherborne.
Walk with the giant on your left down the lane towards Cerne Abbas.

2 Turn left along a lane towards the giant. Ignore a path beside the River Cerne on your right but go across the bridge to a T junction. Turn left to walk for 50 yards (45 m) then turn right up the hedged path opposite a barn.

10 Retrace your steps to the New Inn. Turn left up Duck Street to return to the lay-by at Giant View.

9 Retrace your steps to the church and turn right to pass the Red Lion on your left. Fork left at the New Inn and fork right up Long Street

4 Cross the stile in the fence ahead. Keep straight on towards the barn just to the right of the trees on the horizon.

5 Turn right just before the barn to walk with the hedge on your left. Go ahead through a gate in the corner of the field and turn right immediately to go through a gate and walk with the hedge on your right.

6 Veer left when the fence bears right. Follow the clear track downhill.

7 Cross a stile on your left and bear slightly left across the field to a stile near the sports field. Cross it and turn half right towards the hedge, then turn right to walk with the hedge on your left to reach a gate on your left.

8 Go through the gate and turn right along the road (Alton Lane). This leads to Long Street, Cerne Abbas. Ignore Abbey Court on your right but fork right to the parish church of St Mary. Turn right up Abbey Street. Pass the Town Pond on your right and go on to a gate on your right which leads to the cemetery. Follow the wall on your right and go down to the holy well.

at the telephone box. Opposite Barton Lodge, turn left up the waymarked footpath to see the old Tithe Barn on your right.

heroine of Hardy's *The First Countess of Wessex* had a clandestine rendezvous with her husband here.

G The Tithe Barn was the prototype of the great barn in which Sergeant Troy led the alcoholic revels in *Far from the Madding Crowd*.

Walk 20

DORCHESTER (CASTERBRIDGE)

3 miles (4.8 km) Easy

Dorchester is Hardy's 'Caster-bridge'. It is a very interesting town in its own right, dating back to AD 70, when the Romans estab-lished 'Durnovaria' as the tribal capital of the Durotriges. It is the town in Wessex that is most associated with Hardy. *The Mayor of Casterbridge* was set here, and there is so much to see relating to Hardy that this walk deserves a full day.

A Hardy's memorial statue was sculpted by Eric Kennington. The grass and plants at Hardy's feet symbolise his beloved Egdon Heath. The statue is sited at the start of The Grove, one of Dorchester's avenues or 'walks'. Hardy wrote of 'the ancient defence of the town, planted as a promenade'. Along this walk Henchard tried to persuade Farfrae to remain in Casterbridge in *The Mayor of Casterbridge*.

B High West Street was described by Hardy as 'Timber houses with overhanging storeys, whose small-paned lattices were screened by divinity curtains on a draw string, and under whose barge boards old colonels waved in the breeze'. The Old Tea House, dated 1635, which you pass on your left at the top of the street, still fits that bill.

C Shire Hall is on your right when you turn down Glyde Path Road, or Shire Hall Lane. This is where the Tolpuddle Martyrs (see Walk 29) were tried in 1834. The court was bought by the Trades Union Congress in 1955 and is preserved as a memorial to the Martyrs. Hardy wrote *The Mayor of Casterbridge* in a house, now demolished, in Shire Hall Lane.

D The Hangman's Cottage features in Hardy's short story *The Withered Arm*. It was formerly the home of the notorious Jack Ketch, the man who hanged the Duke of Monmouth's defeated supporters after Judge Jeffreys had sentenced them.

E The path beside the River Frome divides town and country, as Hardy remarked: 'Casterbridge … was a place deposited in the block upon a cornfield. There was no suburb in the modern sense … reapers at work among the sheaves nodded to acquaintances standing on the pavement corner.'

F In Hardy's day, the Town Bridge was built of brick and attracted down-and-outs who accosted passers-by.

G Mill Street was Hardy's Mixen Lane, which consisted 'of thatched and mud walled houses by the sallows … the hiding place of those who were in distress and in debt and trouble of every kind.'

H Hardy liked to visit the old church of St George as he was a friend of the rector's sons. Later, whilst living at Max Gate, he attended services here. The church was built on a Roman cemetery and a first-century Roman tombstone inscribed to the memory of Carinus is preserved on the inner wall of the tower.

There is also a Norman tympanum above the south doorway showing St George slaying the Turks at the Battle of Antioch. Hardy made Elizabeth-Jane meet Lucetta in this churchyard in *The Mayor of Casterbridge*, while nearby, either on Fordington Green (in front of the church) or on the playing-field you pass before Salisbury Terrace, a rough gallows was erected in *The Dynasts*. An effigy of Napoleon was hung from it and set on fire by lighting a pile of wood below it. The flames lit up the 'grey tower of Durnover Church' (St George's church) and when they reached the heart - an animal's bladder filled with gunpowder - the whole effigy exploded.

I The King's Arms was 'the chief hotel in Casterbridge'. Susan Henchard and her daughter Elizabeth-Jane looked through its window to see the husband who had sold her many years before. He was now Mayor of Caster-bridge attending 'a great public dinner of the gentle-people and such like leading folk'.

J Trinity churchyard was overlooked by the seed shop that housed Henchard's last business in Casterbridge.

K The excellent Dorset County Museum includes a reconstruction

DORCHESTER (CASTERBRIDGE)

Continued

0   1 mile
0   1 km

1 Start from the car park at the crossroads known as Top o'Town in Dorchester. The entrance to the car park is 30 yards (27 m) down the A35 towards Bridport, near its junction with the A37 to Yeovil and the A354 to Weymouth, close to the Devonshire and Dorset Regiment Museum.
Walk back to the crossroads and notice Hardy's statue across The Grove (the road to Yeovil) on the left of the roundabout. Go ahead down High West Street.

2 Turn left up Glyde Path Road (also named Shire Hall Lane). When this road bears left, go straight ahead down steps. Pass the thatched 'Hangman's Cottage' on your left, cross the River Frome and turn right along the path beside the river.

3 Cross London Road, passing Town Bridge on your right. Continue along the path with the river on your right, passing the Exhibition Hotel on your left. Pass River Crescent on your left to go ahead up Mill Street. Turn right over the old Bridge opposite the Swan Inn and turn right up Holloway Road.

7 Walk down Weymouth Avenue as far as Maumbury Ring on your left. After visiting this ancient earthwork, walk to the road junction and turn sharply right up Maumbury Road. Immediately after the Great Western Hotel, turn right down a footpath and turn left up West Walks. Keep straight on, passing the old Roman wall on your right, to the roundabout. Turn left, then right for the Top o'Town car park.

4 Turn left up Pound Lane to Fordington High Street and turn left to St George's church. Bear right around the Green to South Walks Road, where you turn right up the track opposite no 27. Go ahead in the shade of an avenue of chestnuts past a playing-field on your right. Continue down Salisbury Terrace, then Salisbury Street, to Town bridge. Turn left up High East Street.

6 Turn left down High West Street, passing the Dorset County Museum and the statue of the Dorset poet and friend of Hardy, William Barnes, on your left. Turn right down South Street. Bear right at the road junction to Weymouth Avenue.

5 Turn right into North Square with St Peter's church on your left. Turn left up Colliton Street and left again down Grey School Passage, passing Trinity church on your left.

of Hardy's study at Max Gate.

L The gossips used to meet near the town pump at the top of South Street. Gabriel Oak dressed in a shepherd's smock for the Candlemas hiring fair here in Far from the Madding Crowd. The Antelope Hotel is where Lucetta met Henchard in The Mayor of Casterbridge.

M A tall brick house on your left, now a branch of Barclay's Bank, was the model for Henchard's house. High on your right, opposite the Hardye Arcade (named after the founder of the grammar school), is a plaque to show where Hardy trained as an architect in Hick's office.

N Maumbury Ring was a Neolithic earthwork adapted by the Romans to form an amphitheatre. Its 'dismal privacy' was used for secret meetings in The Mayor of Casterbridge.

O Henchard found a home for his rediscovered wife and daughter about halfway along West Walks.

Walk 21

THE DORSETSHIRE GAP

2.5 miles (4 km) Moderate

0   1 mile
0   1 km

'The secret of Blackmoor', Hardy wrote in *Tess of the d'Urbervilles*, 'was best discovered from the heights around'. This is a walk along the great chalk ridge that overlooks the Blackmoor Vale, the 'Vale of Little Dairies' where Tess was born. The walk is well off the beaten track. Park your car on the verge near Folly, where Walk 17 also begins. Look out for wild flowers and foxes.

7 Turn left along the road back towards Folly and your car.

Armswell Farm

Nettlecombe Tout
(A)
Fort

P
Folly

Dorsetshire
(B) Gap

6 Keep straight on with a hedge on your right. Pass farm buildings on your right and turn right through a gate, then turn left immediately to follow a fenced track down to the road.

5 Having enjoyed the view, return to the foot of the slope and turn left along the path into the woodland, with steep banks on your left. Go ahead through a gate and continue with trees behind a fence on your left uphill to a gate in the hedge ahead.

4 When a similar sunken track comes in to meet yours from the left, turn left along it to a path junction. This is the famous Dorsetshire Gap. You won't appreciate it until you climb the slope on your left.

3 When the hedge finishes on your left, turn left and walk towards a prominent water-tank. Continue across the field to a small gate in the hedge ahead. Veer slightly right downhill to a gate which leads to a sunken track through woodland. Follow this track which gradually bears right.

1 Park at the roadside north of Folly, which is between Piddletrenthide and Mappowder about 10 miles (16 km) north-west of Dorchester. Walk eastwards along a track which crosses the road, passing a farmhouse on your right.

2 Ignore a greener track which forks to the right (and is followed in Walk 17). When your track turns right, keep straight on uphill with woodland on your left and a fence on your right. Bear left through a gate and turn right immediately along the hedged path.

A Nettlecombe Tout is a fine lookout with a single ancient ditch. The earthwork seems to have been left uncompleted. Tout was a Celtic god, Romanized to Toutates.

It was around here that Tess was compelled to look for work the winter following her desertion by Angel Clare. When Tess came to these uplands, the heights seemed friendly at first: 'In the middle distance ahead of her she could see the summits of Bulbarrow and of Nettlecombe Tout ... They had a low and unassuming aspect from this upland, though as approached on the other side from Blackmoor in her childhood they were as lofty bastions against the sky'.

B The Dorsetshire Gap is a quirk of geology, where many steep slopes meet in a small area, as if a giant had folded the chalk like a pocket handkerchief. The view from the top of the slopes is breathtaking. Hardy described it in *Tess of the d'Urbervilles*: '... the hills are open, the sun blazes down upon fields so large as to give an unenclosed character to the landscape, the lanes are white, the hedges low and plashed, the atmosphere colourless ... in the valley, the world seems to be constructed upon a smaller and more delicate scale; the fields are mere paddocks ... Arable lands are few and limited; with but slight exceptions the prospect is a broad rich mass of grass and trees, mantling minor trills and dales within the major. Such is the Vale of Blackmoor'.

BADBURY RINGS

3 miles (4.8 km) Easy

0 _____ 1 mile
0 _____ 1 km

This is a popular picnic venue, but you can escape the crowds quite easily by following the clear tracks for just a short distance from Badbury Rings. Apart from the ancient monument, this is an oasis of natural downland, having been restored to sheep grazing after scrub clearance carried out by the Prince's Trust in 1984. The sense of history is enhanced by following a Roman road.

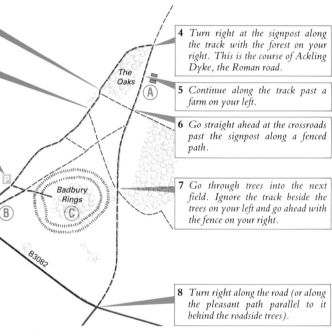

3 *Follow the track into an oak wood. Go straight ahead at the crossing of woodland tracks marked by a signpost and, ignoring cross paths, go to the end of the wood.*

2 *Go ahead through a belt of trees to walk along a fenced track.*

1 *Park in the car park to the left (west) of Badbury Rings, which are signposted on your right as you come along the B3082 4 miles (6.4 km) north-west of Wimborne. Walk away from the Rings along the track with the fence on your left.*

4 *Turn right at the signpost along the track with the forest on your right. This is the course of Ackling Dyke, the Roman road.*

5 *Continue along the track past a farm on your left.*

6 *Go straight ahead at the crossroads past the signpost along a fenced path.*

7 *Go through trees into the next field. Ignore the track beside the trees on your left and go ahead with the fence on your right.*

9 *Turn right at the sign to Badbury Rings, then bear right immediately over a stile beside a gate. Continue past the round barrows on your left. Go ahead to visit the Rings before going through a kissing-gate on your left to the car park.*

8 *Turn right along the road (or along the pleasant path parallel to it behind the roadside trees).*

A This is Ackling Dyke, the Roman road from Dorchester to Old Sarum. It was intersected by a road from Poole Harbour to Bath just to the north-east of the Rings. This is probably the location of the Roman settlement of Vindocladia (White Ditches). The 'agger' or metalled surface of the Roman road stands 6 ft (1.8 m) high and is between 40 feet (12 m) and 50 feet (15 m) wide. Ackling Dyke was probably raised as early as AD 90 and was a great highway for 300 years.

B This is another stretch of Ackling Dyke.

C Badbury Rings is an excellent example of an Iron Age hill fort. It was built by the Veneti not long before the Roman invasion of Britain, and was designed for slingstone warfare. Some of the ditches are more than 60 feet (18 m) deep and may have been nearly twice as deep 2000 years ago. The outermost of its three concentric ramparts is nearly a mile in circumference, so a visit to the Rings can be a walk in itself. Despite achieving the peak of its builder's technology, Badbury Rings was one of the first forts captured by the Second Augustan Legion under Vespasian in either AD 43 or 44.

Walk 23
GOLDEN CAP
3 miles (4.8 km) Strenuous

```
0                                              1 mile
├──────────┼──────────┼──────────┤
0                          1 km
```

This is a walk over the highest cliff on the south coast. The scenery is dramatic and the views are extens- ive. Much of the route is across National Trust property, which means that the land is farmed tradi- tionally, with none of the large ploughed fields and bare barbed- wire fences found elsewhere.

4 *Turn sharply right to follow the signposted bridleway. Keep the hedge on your left until you go through a gate and walk right around the edge of this field to a gate in its far top corner. Follow the signposted bridleway to Langdon Hill, bearing right to a signpost where you turn left, with the fence on your right, to Seatown.*

5 *Go ahead through a gate and bear right along the edge of the wood on Langdon Hill. Turn right at a signpost to follow the path to Seatown, which follows a fence on your left to rejoin the Coast Path at a signpost. Turn left through the scrubland.*

6 *Bear left near the end of this scrubland to a waymarked gate. Follow the yellow arrow to a hedged path ahead. Cross a footbridge to bear right across a field to a waymarked bar stile. Walk down a narrow path to a stile which gives access to Sea Hill Lane. Turn right to reach the car park.*

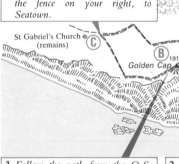

St Gabriel's Church (remains) **C**

Golden Cap **B** 191

Black Covert

Sea Hill Lane

to Chideock

P Seatown **A**

3 *Follow the path from the O.S. triangulation pillar to the memorial stone to the Earl of Antrim. Continue downhill to a signpost, where you bear right to a ruined church (St Gabriel's).*

A Seatown is situated in a gap in the cliffs overlooking a shingle beach. It has an 18th-century inn.

B At 618 feet (188 m), Golden Cap is the highest cliff along the south coast. It is named after its flat summit of golden sandstone. The exhilarating views from the top extend from Chesil Beach and the Isle of Portland in the east to Lyme Regis and Devon in the west. The National Trust has achieved the conservation of 6 miles (9.6 km) of

2 *Walk with the fence on your right, then follow the well-trodden path through scrubland. Cross a bar- stile and bear left along the signposted Coast Path across an open field to a signpost beside a bench. Continue to reach a signposted stile in the fence on your left. Cross it to follow the path to the summit of Golden Cap.*

rugged cliffs in its Golden Cap Estate. Lord Antrim, the chairman of the National Trust from 1966 until his death in 1977, is remem- bered with a memorial at the summit.

C The ruined church at Stanton St Gabriel testifies to the former existence of a thriving community

1 *Start from the car park near the beach at Seatown. This is at the end of Sea Hill Lane, which runs south from the A35 opposite the church in Chideock. This is on the Southern National's 31 & X31 bus routes between Weymouth and Taunton.*
As you face the sea, turn right to keep it on your left. Follow the signposted Dorset Coast Path, which climbs away from the beach towards Golden Cap.

here. There were 23 families living in cottages around the village green in 1650, but the population gradually shifted to nearby Morcombelake. Finally, in 1824, the road was re-routed through Morcombelake.

40

Walk 24
EGDON HEATH
3 miles (4.8 km) Moderate

0				1 mile
0		1 km		

Egdon was the name coined by Hardy for the collection of heaths between his home and Bournemouth. This is its western edge, nearest his birthplace. The landscape of much of Egdon Heath has been radically transformed, being overpopulated in the east and afforested.

5 **Turn right carefully along the road for 200 yards** *(180 m) until the old road enters Puddletown Forest. Veer right along it, parallel to the A35.*

6 Ignore the first track on the right, but turn right at the second and keep on ahead when a track joins yours from the right. Ignore a track from the left, but take the first track on your left at the next crossing point back to the start.

1 Park your car in the signposted car park on your right at the entrance to Puddletown Forest at Beacon Corner, where a minor road from Puddletown bends left. This is 1 mile (1.6 km) south-west of Puddletown, where the A354 joins the A35 and the 184, 187, 188 and 189 buses pass on their way to Salisbury, Weymouth and Bournemouth.
Walk back to the bend in the road and, facing the forest from the direction of Puddletown, go ahead westwards along the forest track signposted 'Yellow Ham Hill'.

2 Turn left uphill through pine trees, ignoring a path that joins yours from the left. Bear right at the next track junction.

4 Take the second track on your right. When this track bends right, look for a yellow arrow waymarking a path through the trees ahead. Bear right along it down to the A35 road.

3 Fork left. Ignore a downhill track on your left but turn right along a green path. Emerge at a crossing point of five tracks and take the second from your left. Fork right only to bear left to a crossing point of 6 tracks.

A Hardy was fascinated by the heath's mysterious round hollows scooped out of the earth and evident here on both sides of the path. He had lain in one as a child, buried among the ferns 'reflecting on his experiences of the world so far as he had got'. Hardy recalled in *The Life* that 'he came to the conclusion that he did not wish to grow up. Other boys were always talking of when they would be men. He did not want at all to be a man.' In his poem *Childhood among the ferns* he said: 'Why should I have to grow to man's estate, in this afar-noised world perambulate?'

B This is the area where 'Mistover Knap', the home of Eustacia Vye was located in *Return of the Native*. Unlike Eustacia, who wanted away to 'the great arteries of the world', Clym Yeobright enjoyed the sights, sounds and smells of the heath as he cut furze: 'Bees hummed around his ears with an intimate air, and tugged at the heath and furze-flowers at his side in such numbers as to weigh them down to the sod ... Tribes of emerald green grasshoppers leaped over his feet, falling awkwardly on their backs, heads, or hips, like unskilful acrobats, as chance might rule; or engaged themselves in noisy flirtations under the fern-fronds with silent ones of homely hue.'

C The old road parallel to the modern A35 is where, beneath the overhanging trees, Hardy places the sad meeting between Troy and the weak and ill Fanny Robin, struggling to reach the workhouse in *Far from the Madding Crowd*.

41

Walk 25
MAX GATE
5.5 miles (8.9 km) Easy

This is a walk rich in associations with Hardy. Max Gate, the home that Hardy designed for himself, is passed, as is Stinsford churchyard, the last resting-place of his heart. The grave of Hardy's great friend William Barnes is visited, while many of the paths followed can be identified in novel, poem or biography. This is also the western end of Hardy's 'Valley of the Great Dairies', where Tess had her happiest days in *Tess of the d'Urbervilles*. After walking out with her Angel in these lush water meadows, Tess marries him in the church that is passed at West Stafford.

A The red-brick, Victorian house of Max Gate can be glimpsed over the wall and through the trees. It belongs to the National Trust, is rented as a private residence and is therefore not open to the public. It was designed by Hardy and was his home for over 40 years. Hardy supervised its building between 1883 and 1885 and he died here on 11th January, 1928. In 1886, Hardy wrote: 'Our life here is lonely and cottage like'. Here he wrote *The Woodlanders* and *Tess of the d'Urbervilles* and much of his poetry. His study from Max Gate has been reconstructed in the Dorset County Museum (see Walk 20). Max Gate proved to be a magnet for his admirers during Hardy's lifetime and the garden door in Sywards Road was Hardy's escape route when he wanted to walk his dog 'Wessex' but avoid the crowds gathered at the front gate. The rich and famous also came here to visit Hardy, including the Prince of Wales and Lawrence of Arabia.

B Hardy's great friend and mentor was William Barnes, the Dorset dialect poet. Barnes left teaching to become the rector at both Whitcombe and Winterborne Came in 1862. Over 20 years later, Hardy was to visit him and talk 'of old families'. This was when Hardy had *Tess of the d'Urbervilles* in mind. William Barnes is buried at the foot of the Celtic cross in the corner of the churchyard. The 13th-century church is dedicated to St Peter at Winterborne Came.

C St Andrew's church, West Stafford, has been identified as the scene of Tess's marriage to Angel Clare in *Tess of the d'Urbervilles*. The three bells of 'Talbothays parish church' were rung for her wedding. One of this church's three bells dates from 1595 and the other two from 1620.

D Stafford House is best seen from the lane leading to Hardy's Cottage. Look right just after crossing the first bridge. It is the 'Frome-Everard' of Hardy's short story *The Waiting Supper* and is described as being 'solidly built of stone in that never-to-be-surpassed style for the English country residence - the mullioned and transomed Elizabethan'.

E This delightful riverside path is the 'embowered path' in *Under the Greenwood Tree*. Hardy's poem *The Dead Quire* tells how phantom singers passed this way to the church at Christmas and disappeared into the churchyard.

F Hardy's grandfather, father and uncle were all in the church choir of St Michael's church, Stinsford. Immortalised by Hardy in *Under the Greenwood Tree* as the 'Mellstock Quire', the choir was replaced by an organ about the time of Hardy's birth. The musicians' gallery was probably removed about 1880. The porch of the church contains a sketch-plan by Hardy showing the shape of the gallery and where each player and singer sat. In the poem *A Church Romance* (subtitled *Mellstock: circa 1835*), Hardy wrote of his mother seeing her future husband in the gallery and falling in love at first sight:

'turned in the high pew, until her sight
Swept the west gallery, and caught its row
Of music-men with viol, book and bow.'

Hardy's heart is buried in the grave of his first wife, Emma. His ashes were interred at Poets' Corner in Westminster Abbey. Hardy wrote *Rain on a Grave* after the death of Emma:

'Soon will be growing
Green blades from her mound.
And daisies be showing
Like stars on the ground.
Till she form part of them -
Ay - the sweet heart of them.'

0   1 mile
0   1 km

6 *Fork right after the bridge to follow the path to Stinsford church. Walk round to the far side of the church to see where Hardy's heart is buried, opposite the seat.*

5 *Turn right along the lane signposted 'Hardy's Cottage'. Just before the bridge to Lower Bockhampton, turn left along the path beside a branch of the River Frome. You come to a bridge over a tributary stream. (Note this bridge, as you will return to it.)*

Stinsford

7 *Retrace you steps to the bridge at no* **5**, *cross it and turn right. Go ahead over a footbridge and follow the well-trodden path to a stile beside a gate. Follow a track under a road bridge and turn left over a brick bridge across the River Frome.*

Lower Bockhampton

River Frome

Dorchester

8 *Turn right at a road, then up the first road on your left. Keep ahead up a path when this road bears right and cross the railway by a bridge. Go ahead to the A352.* **Cross this carefully** *and turn right to reach a roundabout. Turn left through the new housing estate to retrace your steps to St Mary's School and the start in South Court Avenue.*

West Stafford

1 *Park your car at the end of South Court Avenue, which is reached from Maumbury Road in the south of Dorchester.*
Walk eastwards past St Mary's School on your left. Veer left through a new housing estate to reach the A352 at a roundabout. Turn right to cross a bridge over a by-pass. Before a second roundabout, cross the road to Max Gate on your left. Go past Max Gate and turn left up Syward Road to see the door in the wall on your left. Retrace your steps to the A352, and re-cross it.

2 *Go ahead along the footpath to the wood on the horizon, following the hedge on your left. Pass a stile on your left and continue uphill to enter the trees by a stile. Go on downhill to reach a lane. Cross it to follow the track opposite. When it bends right, look for a path to Winterborne Came church on your right. Retrace your steps to the lane and turn right along it to reach the A352. Turn right towards Wareham.*

Came Park

Winterbourne Came

3 *Turn left just before the A352 bears left. Follow the bridleway to West Stafford through a waymarked gate. Walk with the hedge on your left to a little gate ahead. Continue with the hedge on your right and the course of the Winterborne (winter stream) on your left.*

4 *Go through a gate ahead and pass gates in the hedge on your right to reach a gate in the corner of the field. Bear right beside the hedge to a gate which gives access to a track on your right. This leads under the railway. Continue along a track, ignoring a stile into a housing estate on your right. Turn right past the old rectory to St Andrew's church, West Stafford. Turn left along the road just before the church. Cross a bridge over a branch of the River Frome and bear left to a road junction.*

Walk 26
HARDY'S COTTAGE
3.5 miles (5.6 km) Easy

This is a walk through the true heart of Hardy's Wessex, where he was born, grew up and wrote two of his most famous novels - *Under the Greenwood Tree* (1872) and *Far from the Madding Crowd* (1874).

A Thomas Hardy was born in this cottage on 2nd June, 1840. You can view the interior, including the bedroom where Hardy was born, by prior appointment only. Telephone Dorchester (0305) 62366 or write with a SAE to Hardy's Birthplace, Higher Bockhampton, Dorchester, Dorset, DT2 8QJ. You can see the front exterior and garden without an appointment between 11 and 6 (or sunset) from April to October. Hardy's Birthplace is a National Trust property, but it is also the home of its tenants, who act as custodians. On your way in, notice the squint window in the porch where Hardy's grandfather used to watch for Excisemen coming to search for smuggled spirits. The sound of a whiplash on the bedroom window-pane in the early hours of the morning would see Hardy's grandfather going downstairs to bring in tubs of brandy left on the threshold. He would hide these safely away until the smugglers returned to collect them. Hardy's grandmother told young Thomas old tales at the (now restored) great inglenook fireplace. Hardy's grandfather built the cottage in 1800 and in the poem *Domicilium* Hardy recalls his grandmother's account of the place when she first settled there. This was written by the teenage Hardy after his grandmother's death in 1857:
'Our house stood quite alone, and those tall firs
And beeches were not planted.
Snakes and efts
Swarmed in the summer days, and nightly bats
Would fly about our bedrooms.
Heathcroppers
Lived on the hills, and were our only friends;
So wild it was when first we settled here.'

You can also see Hardy's room (shared with his brother Henry). Here he wrote *Under the Greenwood Tree*, in which Hardy's cottage is depicted as the home of Tranter Dewy. 'It was a long low cottage with a hipped roof of thatch, having dormer windows breaking up into the eaves, a chimney standing in the middle of the ridge and another at each end'. On the left is the stone-flagged room with its ceiling bisected by a low beam from which mistletoe hung for the Dewys' Christmas party. Hardy also wrote *Far from the Madding Crowd* here. Today, honeysuckle clambers up the walls and apple trees are scattered on the lawn, as when Hardy was a boy.

B The view of Admiral Hardy's monument must have interested his namesake. Hardy introduced his remote ancestor into his historical novel *The Trumpet Major*.

C Kingston Maurward House is an extravagant manor built close to an older one between 1717 and 1720 by George Pitt, who married Lora Grey, the last heiress of a longstanding local family. It is encased in dressed Portland stone because George III regretted it was 'built of b-b-brick'. The owner went bankrupt to please the King. It is Hardy's 'Knapwater House' of his first published novel *Desperate Remedies*. Miss Aldclyffe lived in it, 'on a hill beside the river'. In real life, here lived Julia Augusta Martin. She founded the village school (Hardy was its first pupil) and took a maternal interest in the young Hardy.

D The old manor-house dates from the late 16th century and is the ruined manor in *Desperate Remedies*.

E The old school house in Lower Bockhampton (Hardy's 'Lower Mellstock') is where Hardy spent his first year at school at the age of seven. He then went to school in Dorchester. Fancy Day was the teacher here in *Under the Greenwood Tree*. On the night of carol singing, young Dick Dewy goes missing and is found leaning against a tree gazing at Fancy's window.

F Thorncombe Wood and Black Heath together form a 66-acre (26.4 hectare) nature reserve. Look for a ridge crossing your path in Thorncombe Wood. This is the course of Ackling Dyke, the

1 *Start from the car park near Hardy's cottage. Coming from Dorchester, follow the A35 road towards Puddletown. After 3 miles (4.8 km), turn right along a lane to Higher Bockhampton. Turn left towards Hardy's cottage, but turn right after 100 yards (90 m) for the car park.*
Follow the signposted woodland path to Hardy's cottage, bearing left uphill from the car park. Ignore a path on your right but continue to a signpost where you turn left, then bear right. Turn left down to Hardy's cottage.

3 *Go through a waymarked gate and follow the well-trodden path straight ahead across the middle of the field to a track where you turn left to reach a minor road.*

4 *Cross the road and continue along the waymarked bridleway ahead. Keep the fence on your right until you go ahead through a gate to walk with the fence on your left. Bear left, whilst overlooking Kingston Maurward Manor on your right. Go through a gate to cross a corner of a field to a gate ahead on your left. Follow a track to a gate which gives access to a lane.*

5 *Turn right to walk past the old Tudor manor on your left. Continue past the demonstration orchard and garden of the Dorset College of Agriculture on your left. Go through a small gate beside a cattle grid. Walk past the bungalows of Knapwater on your left to reach the old school house on your left.*

2 *Turn left around Hardy's cottage to walk down Bockhampton Lane. Pass the turn for the car park on your left and go ahead to the road (Cuckoo Lane). Turn left along it for 50 yards (45 m) then turn right up the waymarked, hedged track*

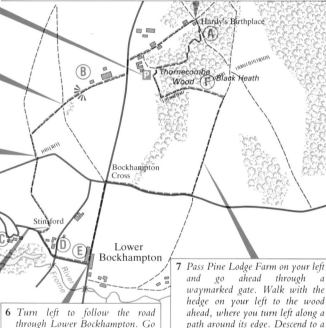

(Hardy's 'drong'). When it bears right, keep straight on through a small waymarked gate into a field to walk with a hedge on your right. Notice the monument to Admiral Hardy straight ahead on the horizon.

6 *Turn left to follow the road through Lower Bockhampton. Go ahead to a crossroads, where you turn right towards Tincleton. Turn left after half a mile (0.8 km) along the track to Pine Lodge Farm.*

7 *Pass Pine Lodge Farm on your left and go ahead through a waymarked gate. Walk with the hedge on your left to the wood ahead, where you turn left along a path around its edge. Descend to a gap in an iron fence and bear left along a track. Pass waymark no 10 but bear right when you reach picnic tables. Pass waymark no 3 to reach the car park.*

Roman road from Durnovaria (Dorchester) to Londinium (London) via Badbury Rings and Old Sarum. The ghost of a Roman centurion has been seen here, his feet elevated to the road's former height.

Walk 27
TOLPUDDLE
5 miles (8 km) Easy

This walk explores the valley of the River Piddle, and the attractive heathy ridge to the south of it, from the village of Tolpuddle - a place made famous by its martyrs, who suffered transportation to Australia in 1834 for daring to form a trade union. Tolpuddle also featured as 'Tolchurch' in Hardy's first published novel, *Desperate Remedies*. Owen Graye was sent to superintend the restoration of the church here, while Manston and the postman fled through the night to Tolpuddle from Wareham, perhaps along the lane where this walk starts and finishes.

A Whether you arrive in Tolpuddle by bus or car, you will soon see evidence of the Tolpuddle Martyrs. Near the bus stop at the Bere Regis end of the village can be seen a plaque on the wall of a cottage. This used to be Thomas Stanfield's cottage and the plaque reads:

'Dedicated by the Trades Union Congress to the memory of the six agricultural labourers of this village whose trade union meetings in this cottage led to their being sentenced to seven years' transportation in 1834.'

They had formed a (legal) Friendly Society of Agricultural Labourers in order 'to preserve ourselves, our wives, and our children from utter degradation and starvation'. They planned, by withholding their labour, to force farmers to increase their wages from eight shillings to ten shillings a week. If you park near the village green you will see the old sycamore tree under which the Martyrs met. A thatched memorial shelter now stands near it. An exhibition about the Tolpuddle Martyrs is housed in one of the six Memorial Cottages at the Dorchester end of the village. They were erected by the T.U.C. in 1934 to mark the centenary of their martyrdom.

Also erected to mark their centenary, unveiled at precisely 4 pm. on 31st August, 1934, was the headstone marking the grave of James Hammett, the only one of the Martyrs to return to Tolpuddle. He was buried in the churchyard in November 1891, having almost reached his 80th birthday. He died in Tolpuddle workhouse and his grave was unmarked for 42 years. This is the church that Owen Graye helped restore in Hardy's *Desperate Remedies*, and it really was restored in the mid-19th century, although the carved Purbeck marble coffin lid of Phillip, a 12th -century priest, survives, as does the 14th-century roof. Hardy's Owen Graye stayed with his sister Cytherea in an old farmhouse nearby while the church was being restored. This farmhouse must have been the Manor House.

At the other end of the village, beyond the bus stop, can be seen the memorial gateway at the Methodist chapel, where George Loveless (the leader of the Martyrs) was a lay preacher. James Loveless, George's brother, was another Martyr, as was Thomas Stanfield's son John. The sixth Martyr was James Brine, while James Hammett had been arrested in mistake for his brother John.

These were hard times in rural Dorset and the ruling class feared riots. They therefore had the six men arrested for administering secret oaths. Brought to trial in Dorchester in March 1834, they were sentenced to seven years' transportation to Australia. They were never violent.

A storm of protests and petitions to Parliament ensued the verdict. A massive trades union rally was held in London and the families of the six, who had been refused parish relief by the magistrates and evicted from their cottages, were helped by a specially set up London Dorchester Committee. Pressure continued until two years after the trial. A threat to indict the king's brother, the Duke of York, for administering secret oaths as Grand Master of the Orange Order led to the king granting the Tolpuddle Martyrs a free pardon. The news took a further two years to reach them (George Loveless read of his pardon in an old newspaper handed down by his master). They finally returned to great celebrations in London. Money was raised to lease two farms for them in Essex, but after six years all except James Hammett emigrated with their families to Canada.

TOLPUDDLE
Continued

0   1 mile
0   1 km

6 *Turn right just before the road to pass the church on your left. At the end of this track, go ahead through a waymarked gate to walk with the hedge on your left. Continue through a waymarked gate (ensure it is shut to prevent cows getting at young trees) to go ahead along a track. When this track bends right, go ahead through a waymarked gate. Proceed to a small gate in the far left-hand corner of this field and bear left to a gate giving access to the lane on your left back to Tolpuddle.*

1 *Start from Tolpuddle village green, where the Martyrs used to meet under the old sycamore tree. If you can't park here, try the Martyrs' Inn. Tolpuddle is on the A35 between Puddletown and Bere Regis. It is served by bus nos 186, 187 and 188.*
Walk away from the village green down the lane towards Southover.

2 *Ignore a waymarked gate on your right, bend left with the lane and turn right. Bear left to pass a thatched cottage on your right and continue along a rough, hedged track. Keep to this track, ignoring all turnings until the track enters the wood ahead.*

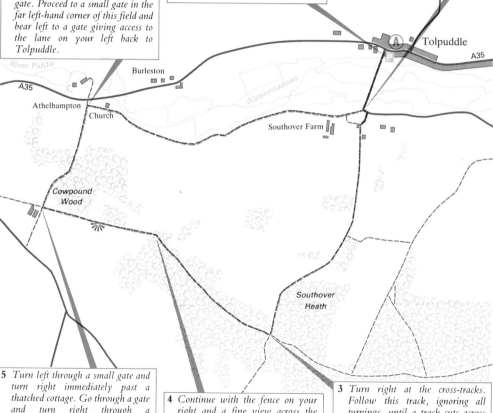

5 *Turn left through a small gate and turn right immediately past a thatched cottage. Go through a gate and turn right through a waymarked gate to walk along the right-hand edge of a field to a gate into the wood. Follow the hollow way, ignoring cross-paths down to Athelhampton.*

4 *Continue with the fence on your right and a fine view across the Frome valley on your left. Pass a conifer plantation on your right. Go ahead through a gate into an oak wood and follow the path near the fence on your left.*

3 *Turn right at the cross-tracks. Follow this track, ignoring all turnings, until a track cuts across from your left. Fork right downhill to walk with a field on your right. Bend left with the track to a gate.*

Walk 28

BERE REGIS

5.5 miles (8.9 km) Moderate

Bere Regis is Hardy's 'Kingsbere sub Greenhill' - 'a little one-eyed, blinking sort of place.' The Saxon queen Elfrida retired to a nunnery here, remorseful after having her step-son Edward murdered at Corfe Castle in 979. Simon de Montfort, the founder of Parliament, also lived here for a while. It is the Tudor heritage that draws the tourists, however. Cardinal Morton lavishly decorated the church, while Henry VIII granted the manor of Bere Regis to Robert Turberville and with it the right of burial in part of the church. Hardy was to give a new twist to this family freehold in *Tess of the d'Urbervilles*. This walk crosses a stretch of Egdon Heath, unspoilt since Hardy's day, to reach the valley of the River Piddle or Puddle. The return to Bere Regis is past the watercress beds where you may see a little diesel engine pulling trucks of watercress along a narrow gauge railway to the packing-shed. Hardy's 'Greenhill' is the Woodbury Hill at the end of this walk, where you can imagine the fair in *Far from the Madding Crowd*. The summit of this hill still retains an ancient earthwork 'in good preservation'.

A The church of St John the Baptist, Bere Regis, is reputedly the most visited church in Dorset. It was fortunate to be spared when most of the village was destroyed by fire in 1788. Two iron hooks, dating from about 1600, hang either side of the church door. They were used to pull burning thatch off the roofs of cottages. The church roof is unique. It was a present from Cardinal Morton to his birthplace in 1425. He became Lord Chancellor of England, Archbishop of Canterbury and chief adviser to Henry VII. The author of 'Utopia', Thomas More (later Sir Thomas More), also grew up in his household.

The most striking features are the 12 figures (apostles?), dressed in Tudor costume, staring down at the congregation. Morton's mother was a member of the Turberville family. So was Jack Durbeyfield in Hardy's *Tess of the d'Urbervilles*. Tess's father, he was convinced that 'there's not a man in the county o' South Wessex that's got grander and nobler skillentons in his family than I'.

The family 'skillentons' lie in the Turberville family vault under a beautiful square-arched Tudor window bearing the Turberville Crest, a 'castle argent', and their arms, 'a lion rampant'. These insignia also appear on a seal and a spoon in the possession of the Durbeyfield family. Tess told Alec d'Urberville about them. When Tess's father dies and the family is evicted, Tess, her mother Joan and the six younger children, fill a hired wagon with all their wordly goods, including a large four-poster bed and move to Kingsbere. Their promised lodgings are already let, however, so the bed is set up beneath the south wall of the church on land that is their freehold, being above the family vault. 'Over the tester of the bedstead was a beautifully traceried window, of many lights, its date being the 15th century. It was called the D'Urberville window'. Inside the church 'within the window under which the bedstead stood were the tombs of the family, covering in their dates several centuries. They were canopied, altar-shaped and plain: their carvings being defaced and broken; their brasses torn from the matrices. The rivet-holes remaining like martin-holes in a sand-cliff.'

Alec d'Urberville may have lain on the altar-tomb of Robert Turberville (Lord of the Manor from 1547 to 1559) under the east window when he pretended to be an effigy. Tess was deceived at first and she afterwards knelt by the large stone in the middle of the aisle (the entrance to the vault) to ask, 'Why am I the wrong side of this door?'

B The standing stone on your left is known as the Devil's Stone. It

C Woodbury Hill is Hardy's 'Greenhill'. Its flat plateau was the site of an annual sheep fair and Gabriel Oak brings Bathsheba's and Boldwood's flocks here: 'Men were shouting, dogs were barking ... but the thronging travellers in so long a journey had grown nearly indifferent to such terrors, though they still bleated piteously'.

0   1 mile

0   1 km

2 Ignore a stile on your right as the road bends left. When the road bends right proceed straight ahead up a footpath past a cemetery on your left. Continue between high hedges to a patch of woodland. Look for blue arrows painted on the trees and bear half-right uphill between two oak trees (the left one has an arrow painted on it). Go ahead along a clear path which veers right through bracken. Continue straight ahead at a cross tracks to pass an old standing stone on your left before another path junction. Continue straight on downhill. Go through an old pollarded oakwood to a hedged track. Bear left as directed by a waymark to pass a farm on your right and reach a lane.

1 Follow the signs to the car park near Bere Regis church. Bere Regis is at the junction of the A35 and the A31 between Dorchester and Bournemouth (and on the 187, 188 and 189 bus routes between these towns).
Visit the church, then bear left from its south porch to a gate leading to the road to Wool. Cross a bridge over watercress beds and turn right up Southbrook.

6 This gate, with a distinctive tree beside it, leads to the old fairground on top of Woodbury Hill (in Hardy's time the 'Nijni Novgorod of South Wessex'). Retrace your steps from here to Bere Regis.

Woodbury Hill

Bere Regis

Black
Hill

Damer
Hill

Blackhill
Clump

Turners Puddle

Little Railway

Yearlings Drove

5 Aim for the church tower as the little railway veers left. Look for a waymarked stile in the fence ahead, near farm buildings on your right. Cross it and veer left to reach the road to Wool again. Turn left towards Bere Regis. Pass the Royal Oak Hotel on your left and cross the road ahead to continue along North Street. Turn right down a path just before Acorn Cottage to reach the A35 road. **Cross this carefully** to go ahead along the waymarked hedged path opposite. Go through a gate and walk uphill with a hedge on your left. Maintain your direction across a track, over a stile, across a field and over another stile down to a lane. Look for another stile opposite and slightly to your right and walk uphill through trees. Cross a stile and bear slightly left to a gate.

to Wool

3 Turn left along this lane and continue for almost 1 mile (1.6 km). Bear left at a junction with a road to Bere Regis but turn right at the next road junction towards Wool. After 300 yards (270 m) you will come to a fork in the road. Don't go ahead along either fork, but turn left along Hollow Oak, a rough track.

4 Walk down to the watercress beds. Cross the narrow gauge railway and a footbridge. Follow the path to Dodding's Farm and turn left as directed by a yellow arrow just after a house on your left. Walk with a fence and the watercress beds on your left. Bear left over a waymarked stile into the next field and walk with the little railway on your left.

Walk 29
LAWRENCE OF ARABIA
6.3 miles (10.1 km) Easy

'Lawrence of Arabia', or T.E. Lawrence, was one of Hardy's most valued friends. He often motorcycled to Max Gate to talk with Hardy, making his last visit in November 1926, before being posted to India. He finally settled on Hardy's 'Egdon Heath' because it reminded him of the desert. The heath is now mostly conifer plantations. The waymarking is excellent when most needed.

A T.E. Lawrence's cottage is in the care of the National Trust and is open on Wednesdays, Thursdays, Fridays, Sundays and Bank Holiday Mondays from 2 to 5 between April and September. It is open between 1 and 4 on Sundays from October to March. Lawrence first rented the cottage whilst serving as 'Private T.E. Shaw' in the Tank Corps at Bovington in 1925. He came here to get away from the camp and work on his 'Seven Pillars of Wisdom'. He wrote: 'I don't sleep here, but come out at 4.30 pm till 9 pm nearly every night, and dream, or write and write or read by the fire, or play Beethoven and Mozart to myself on the box.' His gramophone and typewriter are still here. There was no kitchen. Lawrence enjoyed picnics of 'stuffed olives, salted almonds and Heinz baked beans'. Lawrence later bought the cottage and settled here upon taking his discharge from the Services in 1935.

Lawrence was born at Tremadoc, Gwynedd, in 1888. He was the illegitimate son of Thomas Chapman and the Chapman family nursemaid, Sarah Maden. Unable to marry, his parents changed their names to Lawrence and settled in Oxford, where Thomas Edward was to read history at Jesus College, earning a first-class degree. He had studied the castles in Syria and returned there as an archaeologist.

When the First World War broke out he became an Intelligence Officer, based in Cairo. In 1916 the Arabs revolted against the Turks and the British offered an alliance. Sent to decide which of Grand Sherif Hussein's sons to support, Lawrence chose Feisal and rode with his warriors. His exploits were regarded as of 'inestimable value' by British High Command. His colleagues wrote of his 'gallantry' and his 'brains as well as dash'. He became ashamed of his vanity and for passing on promises that he knew the British would not keep. After the war he worked to see these promises kept. Feisal became King of Iraq and his brother Abdullah became King of Jordan. Although he despised drill and bull, Lawrence sought anonymity by joining the R.A.F. as J.H. Ross in 1922 and then as T.E. Shaw when entering the Royal Tank Corps. He was seen by others as the man to reorganise the RAF in the run-up to the Second World War. On 13th May, 1935, he was severely injured in an accident on his beloved motorcycle. He swerved to avoid two young cyclists as he was returning from Bovington. He died a few days later in Bovington Hospital and was buried at Moreton. After his death Churchill commented: 'I had hoped to see him quit his retirement and take a commanding part in facing the dangers which now threaten the country'. The Greek inscription over the door of his cottage means 'nothing matters'.

B Alderworth is where the cottage Hardy imagined as Clym and Eustacia's home in *The Return of the Native* still stands in the shade of tall Scots pines. Clym found his house 'almost as lonely as that of Eustacia's grandfather, but the fact that it stood near a heath was disguised by a belt of firs which almost enclosed the premises'.

C St Nicholas' church in Moreton was damaged when a German bomb fell in its churchyard in 1940. The replacement windows were engraved by Laurence Whistler in 1958.

D T. E. Lawrence's grave is marked by a stone designed by his friend Eric Kennington, who also sculpted Hardy's statue in Dorchester.

E Bovington Tank Museum is just down the road. It is the largest collection of armoured fighting vehicles in the world. It is open daily all year, while the public can watch mock battles on the last Sunday in July.

LAWRENCE OF ARABIA

Continued

0   1 mile

0   1 km

3 *Continue along the track ahead. Fork left into the wood, passing beehives. Turn right at a yellow arrow on a tree to follow a waymarked path to a stile at the edge of the wood. Maintain your direction, going from stile to waymarked stile, across three fields, then follow a fence and trees on your left to a stile and signpost beside a gate. Turn right along a track to a footbridge and bear right to a second, longer footbridge (over the River Frome). Go ahead to Moreton church and to Lawrence of Arabia's grave.*

2 *Keep straight ahead at a cross tracks and pass a pond on your left. Walk under power-lines and past conifers. Continue through broad-leaved trees to reach a minor road.*

Rimsmoor Pond

Bryants Puddle Heath

Throop Heath

Lawrence of Arabia's Cottage

(A)

Clouds Hill

(P)

(E)

to Bovington

River Frome

Moreton

(D) — Church

(C)

1 *Start from a car park on the east side of the road to Clouds Hill, nearly 1 mile (1.6 km) north of Bovington Camp.*
Walk northwards (right) along the road to pass Lawrence of Arabia's Cottage on your right. Go straight ahead at a T junction as directed by a blue arrow on the roadsign. Veer right to a track between 'Out of Bounds' notices and follow it until a narrow path forks left from it to a road junction. Go ahead along the road opposite. When it reaches a triangle at a crossroads, turn left along a bridleway through the forest.

5 *Turn right along the waymarked track. Fork left as waymarked and follow this track until a yellow arrow points up a track on your left. Turn left along this and fork right after 300 yards (270 m) along a waymarked path. Bear left at the edge of the wood to follow the yellow arrows and the fence back to the road and the car park.*

4 *Retrace your steps to the signpost where you joined the track to Moreton. Continue past it on your left this time, however.*

Walk 30

PUDDLETOWN

5.5 miles (8.8 km) Easy

0   1 mile

0   1 km

Puddletown is the 'Weatherbury' of Thomas Hardy's novel *Far from the Madding Crowd*. This walk takes you to places where scenes in this novel were set and to places associated with its characters. Hardy had relations in Puddletown, the Sparks family, and he often walked to visit them as a child, so he was able to draw on a rich store of memories. The going is easy over wide paths.

> **5** *Walk up the track, passing farm buildings on your right. At the end of the fenced track, turn right through a gate and bear left uphill.*

> **4** *Turn left along this road. Continue for 100 yards (90 m) after passing Waterston Manor on your right, turn left.*

> **1** *Park your car near St Mary's Church, in the centre of Puddletown. This is a village at the junction of the A35 and the A354. The 184, 187, 188 and 189 buses connect it with Salisbury, Weymouth and Bournemouth.*
> *Take the footpath to the right of the church and turn right along the A35, past the school on your right.*

Waterston Manor

B3142

Manor Farm

Watermeadows

Puddletown

A354

Ridge Way

A35

Church

> **6** *Go through a gate ahead and turn left along the ridgeway back to Puddletown. Take care to bear right through the gate at the cross tracks.*

> **3** *Go through a gate ahead and turn sharply right along a bridleway down to the B3142 road.*

> **2** *Pass the bus stop at the end of the village and fork right up the wide, hedged bridleway which runs to the right of a Caravan Club site (not the footpath on your far right). Continue along this bridleway for over 1 mile (1.6 km), ignoring two turnings on your left.*

A Puddletown was a depressed village in Hardy's youth. Rioters had smashed the agricultural machinery that was making them redundant in the 1830's. St Mary's church is the centre of attraction, being the best example of a medieval church in Wessex. There is a 12th-century font, old high box pews and a Musician's Gallery which was erected in 1635. Thomas Hardy's grandfather, when a young man in the late 18th century, played the violoncello here. In 1927, the year before he died, Hardy brought his friend Gustav Holst here. Gabriel Oak, the shepherd in *Far from the Madding Crowd*, sang here. His employer, the woman farmer Bathsheba Everdene, didn't appreciate his sterling qualities until he told her he intended to emigrate. A box pew under the gallery has 'Henery' carved inside it, perhaps inspiring the spelling of Henery Fray, another of Bathsheba's employees.

B The King's Arms is an old coaching inn where George III stopped on his journey to Weymouth.

C This meadow, where in May 'just now every flower that was not a buttercup was a daisy', was the setting of the sheep-washing scene in *Far from the Madding Crowd*.

D Waterston Manor was immortalised as Bathsheba's home.

52

Walk 31
ABBOTSBURY SWANNERY
2.5 miles (4 km) Moderate

0   1 mile
0   1 km

Abbotsbury was Hardy's 'Abbotsea' and 'Abbot's Beach'. Its unspoilt thatched cottages dating from the 17th century made it the ideal location for scenes in the film of Hardy's *Far from the Madding Crowd*. It is a village of great historical interest and is set in the rolling countryside between the Downs and the Chesil Beach. The famous Swannery is open from May to September.

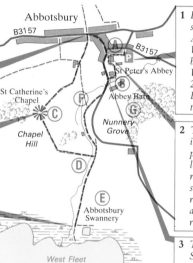

4 *Turn left up Chapel Lane, a rough waymarked track, towards the chapel on the hill ahead. Where Chapel Lane bends right, go ahead through a gate and bear right past farm buildings on your right. Continue uphill through a gate ahead.*

5 *Visit the chapel and bear left to the right-hand edge of a coppice. Descend to a stile in the hedge at the foot of the hill. Go on across a stile in the next hedge and over the chapel withy bed. Turn right to the swannery.*

6 *Walk back past the withy bed to the swannery car park. Follow the track on your left (Grove Lane) past the old mill. Continue to the mill pond and retrace your steps to the car park.*

1 *Park your car in the car park signposted on your left as you enter Abbotsbury on the B3157 from Weymouth. There are infrequent buses to Abbotsbury from Weymouth and Bridport (nos 60 & 210), and Dorchester (no 61). Leave the car park by the walled track towards the church.*

2 *Turn left through a kissing-gate into the churchyard. Turn right to pass the church on your left. Turn left around the church and fork right to a small gate. Continue to a stile, which you cross to see all that remains of Abbotsbury Abbey. Go ahead to the old mill pond and turn right to a lane.*

3 *Turn right up this lane (Church Street) to the village. Bear left up Market Street.*

A Notice two mediaeval stone coffins in the churchyard opposite the porch of St Nicholas' Church. The porch contains the carved effigy of an abbot dating from about 1200.

B South of the churchyard gate is the Pynion End, the best part of the abbey remains. This wall dates from about 1400 and incorporates a fireplace. The Benedictine abbey of St Peter was founded in 1026 by Orcus, King Cnut's steward. It was dissolved in 1539 and sold to Sir Giles Strangways. Abbotsbury is reputed to be one of the oldest centres of Christianity in Britain.

C St Catherine's Chapel was retained as a landmark for sailors after the dissolution. The monks had formerly kept a fire burning here. The chapel is built entirely of stone, roof and all, with heavy buttresses and thick walls. The view is magnificent.

Women came here to pray for 'A husband, St Catherine. A nice one, St Catherine. And soon, St Catherine.'

D The withy bed is where willow is grown to be pollarded annually when the 6 ft (1.8 m) stems are used to tie up reed bundles.

E The swannery was established by the monks in the 14th century. It is at the western end of the brackish water of the Fleet and is protected by Chesil Beach. About 600 mute swans breed here. Come in June and you will see their cygnets.

F The building with a millstone against its wall was the abbey mill.

G The tithe barn is the largest in Britain. Built by the abbey in the 14th century, it is now used as a store for thatching reeds from the Fleet.

Walk 32
THE HARDY MONUMENT
3.5 miles (5.6 km) Moderate

0 _____ 1 mile
0 _____ 1 km

Splendid views, unspoilt heathland and an unusual monument combine to make this an especially attractive walk. The monument is to 'the other Hardy', Sir Thomas Masterman Hardy, Nelson's flag captain at Trafalgar, born at Portesham in 1769.

1 Park your car below the Hardy Monument, which is by the road between Martinstown and Portesham. If you travel by bus (60 or 210 from Weymouth or Bridport, start this walk at Portesham).
With your back to the monument and the sea in front of you, bear left along a distinct path through the heather down to conifers.

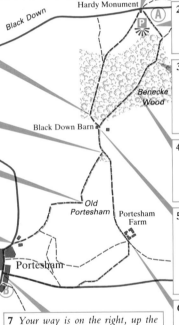

11 Bear right along the uphill path through the trees, ignoring tracks on your right until a right fork is signposted 'Hardy Monument ½'. Go ahead to the monument and car park.

10 Turn left along the track you followed on your outward journey. This time, however, fork left at the bottom gate to a second signpost.

9 Turn left along the walled track at the top of the field. Soon bear right to a gate, where the Hardy Monument can be seen ahead. Continue with the wall on your right to a gate in the corner of the field.

8 Fork right along the bridleway signposted 'Hardy Monument 1½'. Go along a hedged track to a gate then keep to the left side of a field. Follow the distinct track as it swings right.

2 Descend through the trees to a level path. Turn right along this. Look for a blue arrow waymark where you fork left to a forest track.

3 This track bears right uphill. Look for a waymarked path through the trees on your left just before the track bears left. Follow the waymarked path to rejoin the track.

4 Stick to the waymarked track, ignoring a path which forks right. Go ahead at a cross tracks at the edge of the forest to descend to a signpost.

5 Turn left and go through a gate uphill with a fence on your left and a wall on your right. Pass a gate and trees on your right and go ahead through a gate. Continue with a fence on your left and a wall on your right.

6 Pass a farm on your left, go through a gate ahead to follow a track which bends right downhill to a road. Turn right to reach Portesham.

7 Your way is on the right, up the road signposted to Hardy's Monument. First, however, visit Portesham church on your left. Bear right past Portesham Stores.

A The Hardy Monument was erected between 1844 and 1846 (Admiral Hardy died in 1839) and is an ugly octagonal tower over 70 ft (21 m) high. The view from here is magnificent. On your extreme right is Start Point on the south Devon coast, while the Needles can be seen on your extreme left.

B St Peter's church, Portesham, has an interesting epitaph on the outside referring to the Civil War:
'William Weare lies heere in dust,
As thou, and I, and all men must;
Once plund'red by Sabaean force,
Some cald it war, but others worse.

With confidence he pleads his cause
And King's, to be above those laws.
September's eyghth day died hee.
When neare the date of 63.
          Anno Domini 1670'.

Walk 33
MAIDEN CASTLE
2 miles (3.2 km) Easy

This walk is through a page of the unwritten history of Wessex. Maiden Castle is one of the greatest Iron Age hillforts in Britain. It has triple banks and ditches enclosing 45 acres (18 hectares). It was at its peak in the final century before the Roman invasion, when it was the chief settlement of the Durotriges, the tribe which held Dorset. They were prosperous, with wheat production then rivalling yields attained in the Second World War. About 5000 of them lived in this hillfort. Excavators have found traces of their huts and numerous grain storage pits. Their defences were the peak of Iron Age technol-

ogy, perhaps earning the hillfort its 'maiden' label for impregnability. Their chief weapon was the sling and an ammunition stockpile totalling 54,000 pebbles from Chesil Beach has been found. Their wealth tempted the Roman imperialists, however, who fired ballistae at the defenders and locked shields above their heads to reach the gates, which they smashed with battering-rams. Once inside, an indiscriminate slaughter of the inhabitants ensued. In AD 70 the new town of Durnovaria (Dorchester) was built nearby and peace returned to this hillside.

Hardy called the hillfort 'Mai-

Dun'. From its 'huge dimensions and many ramparts'. Henchard, 'glass in hand', often watched his step-daughter and Farfrae out walking in *The Mayor of Casterbridge*. From here he also saw the return of Newson. It is the scene of the story *A Tryst at an Ancient Earthwork*, unsurpassed as an evocation of place and mood. 'It may be likened', wrote Hardy, 'to an enormous many-limbed organism of an antidiluvian time, lying lifeless, and covered with a thin green cloth, which hides its substance, while revealing its contours.'

Finds from the site can be seen in the Dorset Museum (Walk 20).

1 *Start from the car park at Maiden Castle, which is signposted from the A354 on the southern outskirts of Dorchester.*

Walk along the track to enter the hillfort through a maze of banks and ditches.

2 *Go ahead from the gateway across the interior, bearing slightly left to reach a hollow which once contained a dew pond.*

5 *Pass a circular hollow thought to mark a well on your right, with the southern ramparts on your left. Continue along these ramparts. Turn left through the western entrance and retrace your steps to the car park.*

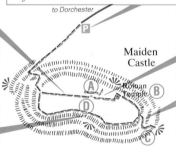

3 *Cross the bank barrow ahead and veer slightly left to see the remains of a Romano-British temple. Continue along the top rampart, with its excellent view over Dorchester, on your left.*

4 *Inspect the double gateways at the eastern entrance to the hillfort. Continue along the southern ramparts.*

A You cross the ditch and bank of an earlier, simpler earthwork that enclosed just 10 acres (4 hectares) at the eastern end of Maiden Castle.

B This Romano-British temple dates from about AD 370.

C The most dramatic moment in Maiden Castle's history came shortly after the Roman invasion of AD 43. The Second Augusta legion, commanded by Vespasian (who became emperor in AD 69), captured the hillfort. Excavations by Sir Mortimer Wheeler in the 1930s uncovered evidence of a

fierce battle in AD 69 at the east gate, where elaborate outworks had been added in 20 BC.

D The separate ramparts have a relationship of distance and height to each other that was carefully calculated and engineered.

Walk 34
MOONFLEET
4 miles (6.4 km) Easy

This is a walk of special interest to children, since it explores the setting of a children's classic: *Moonfleet*, by John Meade Falkner. It is a tale of smuggling on this coast involving the local Mohun family. Thomas Hardy's own grandfather was involved in the smuggling business, which was a common activity in these parts, especially with the increase of excise duties. Meade Falkner had plenty of facts to base his story on. The collector of Customs at Weymouth reported in 1717:

'Tidewaiter Edward Thorne and two assistants arrived near Fleet in the early hours to investigate a reported landing on the Chesil Beach. They were met by thirty men in disguise armed with clubs and other weapons who drove them from the place'. Sixty-nine men and women from along the Fleet were imprisoned at Dorchester between 1800 and 1821 for evading customs, including Joseph and Thomas Zealy from Fleet itself.

A Little remains of the original hamlet of East Fleet, since it was virtually destroyed by a terrible storm on 23rd November, 1824. So strong was the wind that the Ebenezer, a 90 ton sloop, was blown on to the crest of the Chesil Beach, and a mighty tidal wave crashed through East Fleet, destroying the cottages and the nave of the old church. An eye-witness reported that 'the sea began to break over the beach at 5 am. The water came up as fast as a horse could gallop ... The nave of the church was undermined and demolished, also a cottage hard by and another at the end of Butter Street. Two cottages near the garden of the old Priest's house were also thrown down. Two old ladies living in the Priest's house were rescued from a bedroom window. A hayrick was swept away and seven large fishing boats were washed far inland.' The chancel of the old church was spared. Beneath it is the Mohun family vault with the old smugglers' secret passage. Look for a brass plaque on the south wall commemorating John Meade Falkner. The Mohun family are also remembered here with two fine brass plaques. Robert Mohun acquired Fleet in 1566. His son, Maximilian, probably rebuilt the church to incorporate the family vault. The Mohuns were Royalists who had their estate confiscated in the Civil War, although it was returned to them at the Restoration. They remained loyal to the Stuarts even when William of Orange landed.

Robert Mohun (born 1715) was the last male heir and Fleet passed by marriage to the Gould family. The heir to their fortune in 1818 was the bachelor Reverend George Gould, who was Rector of Fleet when the great storm destroyed his church. *The Sherborne Mercury* wrote:
'The Reverend George Gould, Rector of Fleet, a village destroyed by the late storm, intends building a new village; and with a degree of philanthropy that will ever immortalise his name, has taken and provided for all the sufferers under his roof.' *Moonfleet* was published a year after the Gould family line died in 1897.

B The Fleet is a lagoon between the mainland and Chesil Beach. It is a shallow stretch of water containing a lot of weed. Eels, bass and mullet abound, but may only be fished by a few locals. The Fleet has been a protected reserve since the 14th century. The east end of the Fleet is salty and tidal, but it becomes brackish and still in the west.

C The Chesil Beach is a barrier of pebbles connecting the Isle of Portland with the mainland. It is over 17 miles (27 km) long and the stones increase in size towards the east. Some of the stones are as big as saucers near Portland, while they are considerably smaller near Abbotsbury. The Isle of Portland acts as a huge groyne to prevent the pebbles moving on.

D Part of the Moonfleet Hotel was the Mohun family manor house.

E Fleet's new church was built at the vicar's expense between 1827 and 1829. It contains the old church bell.

0   1 mile

0   1 km

5 *Veer right to cross a signposted stile and walk with the wall on your right to another Coast Path signpost. Leave the Coast Path here by turning right over a stile, then immediately right for a few paces to turn left over a stile. Follow this signposted footpath with the hedge on your left. Reach ·a stile in the corner of the field and go ahead with the hedge on your left to another stile.*

6 *Enter a camping and caravan site and keep the hedge on your left until the path turns left to leave the hedge on your right and the camp shop on your left. Walk past a children's playground on your right to a stile in the fence ahead. Turn right along a track which bears left to a lane. Turn left down this lane back to the car park or bus stop.*

1 *Park your car at Holy Trinity Church, Fleet (donation). This church is on your right as you drive along the lane to Fleet from the B3157 at Chickerell, a north-western suburb of Weymouth, well-served by town buses. If you come by bus, walk down the lane from Chickerell towards Fleet, but start the walk at no **2** instead of turning right for the church.*
If you drive to the church, walk back down the lane to the corner where it turns left.

West Fleet
Farm

to Chickerell →

Ⓓ
Moonfleet

Chesil

Ⓒ

Beach

Fleet
Ⓟ Ⓔ

Ⓐ
East Fleet

Ⓑ
The Fleet

4 *Ignore a stile on your right and bear left along a hedged path. Continue across a footbridge. Ignore a stile immediately on your left but cross the field ahead, bearing slightly right towards Moonfleet Hotel. Walk with the fence on your left to a stile and a Coast Path signpost. Pass a notice-board about the Fleet Sanctuary on your left. Descend to the beach at Gore Cove.*

3 *Ignore a stile (signposted to Weymouth) on your left but cross a stile beside a gate on your right to walk with the Fleet lagoon and Chesil Beach on your left. Continue over a stile and a footbridge along a narrow hedged path to a second field. Walk along this coastal path until you reach a footpath signpost.*

2 *From Fleet church, turn right along the signposted path to Old Fleet Church. If you have walked from the bus stop at Chickerell, go straight ahead, passing cottages on your right, then go through a gate on your right to visit the old church.*
Return to the path and continue over a waymarked stile beside a gate. Bear right around the churchyard wall to a footpath signpost where you bear left towards Langton Herring.

Walk 35
WHITE HORSE HILL
4.5 miles (7.2 km) Moderate

```
0                              1 mile
|----+----+----+----+----|
0              1 km
```

The white horse of this walk is a carving of King George III on horseback. He is depicted moving away from his favourite resort of Weymouth.

1 *Park your car near the mill pond at Sutton Poyntz. You can get here by taking the A353 from Weymouth to Preston; turn left at the Ship Inn, then fork right to the Springhead Inn. There is an infrequent bus service from Weymouth to here and a frequent bus service (A) between Weymouth and Preston.*
Cross the bridge upstream of the pond and turn left to pass the pond on your left. Continue along the path beside the stream to the mill.

4 *Turn right through a waymarked gate. Ignore a gate on your left beside a signpost and walk with a fence on your left and a fine view across the bay to Portland on your right. Your path goes ahead from the next gate, but divert right immediately after it to see the white horse which is carved on the hillside. Return to your path to walk with a hedge on your left along the top of the field to a gate ahead.*

5 *Bear right along the track downhill to the village of Osmington below. Return to the footpath signpost, on your left as you come from the village, where the road and houses end. Turn left through the gate towards Sutton Poyntz. The hedge is on your left and a stream (the Jordan) on your right, with the white horse on the hillside behind. Cross the Jordan in the corner of the field and bear right through a gate into the next field, with the White Horse ahead.*

6 *Bear slightly right across the field to bar stiles. Continue to a gate and across the corner of a field to another gate. Keep the hedge on your left as you go through three more gates. Go through a fourth gate to a lane leading back to the start.*

White Horse Hill

156
East Hill

Sutton Poyntz

2 *Turn left over the footbridge and go along the lane between the mill and the millhouse with old millstones set in your path. Turn left around the mill and walk past the pond again towards the Downs ahead. Turn right along the signposted path and turn left through Hunt's Timber Yard.*

3 *Cross a stile to go ahead across the field to a stile in its far right corner. Bear slightly right uphill to a gate and follow the path which bears slightly left to the top of the down. Pass a tumulus on your left.*

Osmington

A The atmosphere and setting of Sutton Poyntz, if not its precise location, is that of 'Overcombe' in Hardy's *The Trumpet Major*.

B Anne Garland watched the review of the troops from here.

C The White Horse covers more than an acre.

D John Constable, the artist, brought his wife to Osmington for their honeymoon.

Walk 36
DURDLE DOOR
2.8 miles (4.5 km) Moderate

This walk follows a section of the Dorset Coast Path which includes Durdle Door, reckoned by many to be the highlight of this coastal walk. The return route is along downland paths which are frequented by chalkhill blue butterflies in the summer, while you may even spot the rare golden-coloured Lulworth skipper. The views are tremendous, from Portland Bill in the west to St Aldhelm's Head in the east.

4 *Fork left uphill along the path to the caravan site. A fence joins your path from the right. Ignore a stile in it, but go through a gate ahead.*

5 *Just before you reach the caravan site, turn right over a stile beside a gate. Bear left to walk beside the hedge on your left. Continue with the fence on your left, crossing three waymarked stiles.*

6 *Ignore a stile on your left which is signposted to West Lulworth youth hostel. Continue to Lulworth Cove car park.*

West Lulworth

B3070

Hambury Tout

Durdle Door

(B)

St Oswald's Bay

P

(A)

Lulworth Cove

3 *Retrace your steps past Durdle Door, now on your right, to a low waymark stone.*

2 *Cross a stile beside a gate where a sign warns you against camping. Bear left along the track to the top of the cliff. This is the Dorset Coast Path, which you follow*

(with the sea on your left) for 1 mile (1.6 km) until you see the natural arch of Durdle Door, jutting out towards Portland across Weymouth Bay.

1 *Start from the car park at Lulworth Cove, which is also the bus stop for the Dorset Queen service no 220 between Dorchester and Coombe Keynes (Wednes-*

days, Fridays and Saturdays only). Lulworth Cove is at the end of the B3070, 5 miles (8 km) south of Wool.
Walk out of the car park, with Lulworth Cove behind you, along a clear, chalky, track.

A Lulworth Cove can be seen as you rest or look back on your initial climb up the path to the cliff-top from the car park. It features in Hardy's writings as 'Lulwind Cove' and is where the dashing but ruthless Sergeant Troy is thought to have drowned in *Far from the Madding Crowd*. Here, too, the drowned bodies of Stephen Hardcombe and his cousin's wife were cast ashore in *A Few Crusted Characters*. Owen and his sister, Cytherea Graye, made an excursion to here from Weymouth in *Desperate Remedies*, Hardy's first published novel.

The most intriguing reference is in *A Tradition of 1804*. Hardy has Solomon Selby, a shepherd's son, see two French generals arrive on a reconnaissance trip for the invasion of England. Solomon recognised one as Napoleon Bonaparte himself. According to legend, the Emperor was overheard by a local farmer's wife who had learnt French in order to help with her father's china business. This lady was born in 1784 and lived to be 104. Keats, the poet who left England for Italy dying of consumption, spent his last hours on English soil here when his ship called by in 1820.

B The natural rock archway of Durdle Door was referred to by Hardy in *The Bird-Catcher's Boy*.

Walk 37

CORFE CASTLE

3.5 miles (5.6 km) Moderate

The ruins of Corfe Castle are a splendid sight, guarding the only gap in the Purbeck Hills. Hardy knew this area well and found an easy intimacy with the past here. Corfe Castle was the Corvsgate that Ethelberta rode to on her donkey from Swange in *The Hand of Ethelberta*.

4 *Turn right along the ridge path. Go through a gate and walk with a fence on your right to a stile beside a gate ahead. Continue, with trees across the field on your left, towards two round barrows ahead.*

5 *Follow the path beside the fence on your right to a gate. Bear right downhill to the bottom bridleway. Turn left along it, with a fence on your right, all the way to a lane. Turn left over a bridge.*

6 *Turn right along a footpath with Corfe Castle above on your left. Emerge near the castle entrance. Turn right past the Cross for West Street. Pass the entrance to the Model Village and continue to the car park.*

Knowle Hill

(A)

(B)
West Hill

East Hill

Church
Knowle

Castle

(D)

Corfe
Castle

A351

(P)

3 *Turn left along the bridleway, waymarked with a blue arrow. Keep to this bottom track, with the hedge on your left, through two gates and wooden bars in a gateway, until a stile beside a gate on your left invites you to Church Knowle. Instead of going left to the church, however, bear right uphill. Cross a stile and continue to the ridge.*

2 *Cross the bridge and bear left to a stile beside a gate in the fence on your right. Go ahead with a ditch on your right before bearing right to a stile beside a gate giving access to a lane. Turn left and proceed for 30 yards (27 m), then turn right over a stile. Go ahead uphill to another stile.*

1 *Park in the car park signposted off West Street, Corfe Castle, which is on the A351 between Wareham (nearest British Rail station) and Swanage, on the 142, 143 and 144 bus routes between Poole and Swanage.*
Look for a stile on your right from the car park and follow its yellow waymark arrow down to a footbridge over the River Corfe.

A A famous ley line runs through tumuli on Knowle Hill and the northern side of Corfe Castle. It strikes the southern side of the northern one of these two tumuli (the round barrow furthest on your left).

B Here is another tumulus on the Corfe Castle ley line.

C The ruins of Corfe Castle dominate this very popular tourist village. The ruins are fundamentally Norman, but this was the site of a Saxon lodge where the scheming Elfrida had her step-son Edward the Martyr murdered in 978. The Saxons were punished for this crime with the rule of Elfrida's natural son, Ethelred the Unready. King John extended and improved the Norman castle in the early 13th century and starved to death 22 French prisoners here. Queen Elizabeth I gave it to Sir Christopher Hatton, one of her court favourites and a Lord Chancellor in the 16th century. Sir John Bankes, Attorney-General to King Charles I, purchased the castle eight years before the Civil War. This conflict brought Corfe Castle's finest hour, but resulted in it becoming another of the castles which Cromwell 'knocked about a bit'. The resolute Lady Bankes twice withstood sieges before her tiny garrison was forced to surrender in 1646.

D The village to the south of Corfe Castle was the centre of Purbeck's stone and marble industry in the Middle Ages.

Walk 38
OLD HARRY
4 miles (6.4 km) Easy

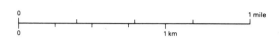

This is a clear, waymarked walk offering fine views and excellent chalk cliff scenery, including the natural arch of Old Harry and the stump of his wife at Handfast Point. The white cliffs between here and Ballard Point (Hardy's Bollard Head) are described in *The Hand of Ethelberta*. In the final stages of this novel, Hardy writes of the steamer 'Spruce' avoiding 'a corner called Old-Harry Point, which lay about halfway along their track, and stood, with its detached posts and stumps of white rock; like a skeleton's lower jaw, grinning at British navigation.' Hardy and Emma lived in Swanage (the Knollsea of Hardy's novels) soon after their marriage in 1875 and they must have walked these cliffs frequently.

1 Studland is at the end of the B3351, which leaves the A351 at Corfe Castle. A minor road (and no. 150 bus) connects it with Swanage and Sandbanks Ferry. Follow signs to South Beach Car Park, near Bankes Arms Hotel. Turn right from this car park along the road past the hotel until the road bends right.

2 Turn left to follow the blue arrows which mark the Dorset Coast Path to Old Harry. Follow this path, with the sea on your left, for 2 miles (3.2 km).

Old Harry Rocks

Parson's Barn

The Pinnacles

Studland

Church

Ballard Down

Ballard Point

8 Turn right along the road back to the car park (turn left for the bus stop).

7 Cross a road to walk up to the church. Go ahead through the churchyard.

6 Go through a gate to continue along a lane, ignoring left turnings.

5 Turn right off the ridge track to go through a gate and follow the blue arrow down to Studland.

4 Continue through a gate in the direction of the obelisk.

3 Bear right along the uphill track to the top of the ridge of Ballard Down, with its view of Poole Harbour on your right (and Swanage on your left).

A Old Harry is the bigger and closer of the two rocks at the end of Handfast Point. It is also distinguished by its natural arch. The stump further out to sea is Old Harry's Wife. On a clear day you can see the Needles and the Isle of Wight from here.

B The two further chalk stumps off the shore walking south of Old Harry are known as the Pinnacles. A sea cave beneath the water between them is called Parson's Barn on account of its huge size, like a tithe barn. These are textbook examples of coastal erosion.

C The church of St Nicholas in Studland is almost entirely Norman. Grotesquely carved faces run along the north and south walls of the nave. Its chalice-shaped font dates from the 12th century, but the carved cross outside is modern, even showing the Concorde airliner.

Walk 39

ST ALDHELM'S HEAD

5.5 miles (8.8 km) Strenuous

```
0                                    1 mile
|----|----|----|----|----|----|
0                          1 km
```

This is a dramatic coastal walk around the 350 feet (105 m) high St Aldhelm's (or St Alban's) Head. There are magnificent views of the Dorset coast, while the large cliffside quarries which provided Purbeck stone for London can be visited (**take great care at the quarries. DO NOT enter them**). Bats inhabit the unsafe caverns now. Puffins and orchids may be seen on this walk.

1 *Park at the car park on your right as you enter Worth Matravers from Corfe Castle. This is on a minor road off the B3069, which leaves the A351 (Poole-Swanage road) at Corfe Castle.*
Turn right from the car park towards the centre of the village, where there is a bus shelter (no. 144 bus between Poole and Swanage) near a duck pond.

2 *Follow the road, which is a short cul-de-sac, opposite the bus shelter. Very soon you turn left along a waymarked path between gardens to a stile. Go ahead across a dry valley to a stile and continue to another waymarked stile. Bear right downhill to a signposted stile.*

3 *Follow the clear path on your right down this valley. Cross a plank to walk with the stream on your right and keep to the track down to the sea. The path is now waymarked by small stone posts that mark the Dorset Coast Path.*

4 *This route turns right with the Coast Path as waymarked to Winspit. Before climbing this steep path, however, continue towards the sea, ignoring the waymarked Coast Path to Dancing Ledge on your left, to see the limestone quarries and the cliffs at Seacombe.*

5 *Retrace your steps from Seacombe to turn left along the Dorset Coast Path towards Winspit, with the sea on your left. Follow the clear path along the cliffs to Winspit, where you descend bearing right and go up the opposite side to bear left back to the cliff edge. Continue to St Aldhelm's Head, where there is a coastguard lookout and a 12th-century chapel.*

Worth Matravers

Chapman's Pool

Seacombe Bottom

Seacombe Cliff

Emmetts Hill

Winspit

St Aldhelm's Chapel

St Aldhelm's Head

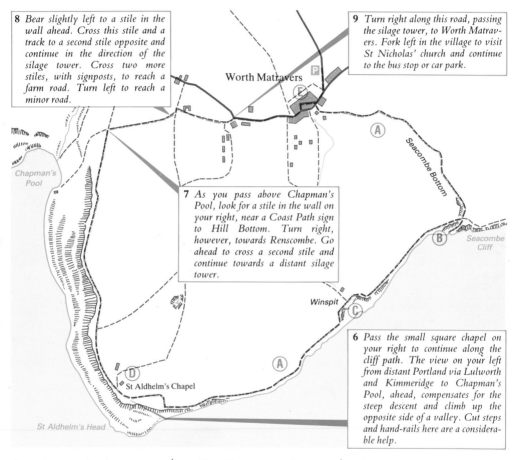

8 *Bear slightly left to a stile in the wall ahead. Cross this stile and a track to a second stile opposite and continue in the direction of the silage tower. Cross two more stiles, with signposts, to reach a farm road. Turn left to reach a minor road.*

9 *Turn right along this road, passing the silage tower, to Worth Matravers. Fork left in the village to visit St Nicholas' church and continue to the bus stop or car park.*

Worth Matravers

Chapman's Pool

7 *As you pass above Chapman's Pool, look for a stile in the wall on your right, near a Coast Path sign to Hill Bottom. Turn right, however, towards Renscombe. Go ahead to cross a second stile and continue towards a distant silage tower.*

Seacombe Bottom

Seacombe Cliff

Winspit

6 *Pass the small square chapel on your right to continue along the cliff path. The view on your left from distant Portland via Lulworth and Kimmeridge to Chapman's Pool, ahead, compensates for the steep descent and climb up the opposite side of a valley. Cut steps and hand-rails here are a considerable help.*

St Aldhelm's Chapel

St Aldhelm's Head

A Notice strip lynchets at these places. These worn terraces are evidence of farming in the Middle Ages, when the land was ploughed in strips and steep banks were formed.

B Seacombe quarries are too dangerous to enter but are impressive enough from the outside. The Jurassic limestone from here and Winspit was used to build the public buildings of 17th century London.

C Winspit also had large quarries.

D St Aldhelm's Head is named after the first Bishop of Sherborne, who was appointed in 705. An anchoress used to serve in the 12th-century chapel. The use of radar was pioneered here in World War II.

E The church at Worth Matravers is dedicated to St Nicholas, the patron saint of sailors.

Walk 40
PORTLAND
2.5 miles (4 km) Easy

The Isle of Portland is not really an island, since it is connected to the mainland by Chesil Beach. It has a character all of its own, however. It was Hardy's 'Isle of Slingers'.

1 *Avoid congestion and road-walking by taking one of the frequent buses from Weymouth to Portland Museum.*
From the Portland museum bus stop, go down Church Ope Road, passing the side entrance to the museum on your left. The road becomes a footpath which passes Rufus Castle on your right. Go down steps towards the beach. When the steps turn left (near a bench) turn right along a narrow, hedged path.

6 *Turn left along a signposted footpath. Bear right towards the cliffs. Walk with the sea below you on the left. Reach the road at a sharp bend. Bear right to reach the bus stop or car park near the war memorial. Enjoy the spendid view from here while you wait.*

5 *Turn left along the third road on your left (the main road through the village of Reforne). Pass the George Inn on your left to reach St George's church at the head of the road. Turn right along Wide Street for 150 yards (135 m).*

4 *Turn left along the track to an old windmill. Fork right to a second old windmill. Bear right, then turn left beside the line of a dismantled railway. Pass a school on your left. Cross a road to continue along a path ahead which reaches the corner of a road at a footpath signpost.*

3 *Turn right along Weston Street for 250 yards (225 m). Turn right along a signposted footpath, with a hedge on your left. Pass an old quarry on your right.*

2 *Go up steps past the ruins of St Andrew's church. Turn right under an old arch and continue through trees. Pass Pennsylvania Castle on your left. Turn left along the road.*

A Portland Museum is partly housed in Avice's Cottage, a 17th century building which features in Hardy's novel *The Well Beloved*.

B In *The Well Beloved*, Jocelyn Pierston often 'paced down the lane to the Red King's castle'.

C Church Ope Cove is the only natural landing-place on the island.

D Jocelyn sealed his engagement to the first Avice in *The Well Beloved* with a kiss among the ruins of St Andrew's church.

E Pennsylvania Castle is Hardy's 'Sylvania Castle', which Jocelyn rented to be near Avice.

F The George Inn was where the 'Court Leet' (local council) met.

G Jocelyn first saw the second Avice in the churchyard of St George's 'where the island fathers lay'.

H Jocelyn walked here with Marcia.